MAKING AN IMPACT

MAKING AN IMPACT

Harvey Thomas
with Liz Gill

A Graham Tarrant Book

DAVID & CHARLES
Newton Abbot London

Jacket photographs by kind permission of the following: *The Press Association Ltd* (Margaret Thatcher); *Popperfoto/Reuter* (George Bush); *Express Newspapers* (Billy Graham); *Financial Times* (Harvey Thomas)

The authors and publishers gratefully acknowledge permission to reproduce the definition of 'Advance man' from *The Longman Register of New Words* Vol 1, 1989, by John Ayto, published by Longman.

British Library Cataloguing in Publication Data

Thomas, Harvey
  Making an impact.
  1. Business firms. Management. Information.
  Information. Presentation – Manuals
  I. Title II. Gill, Liz
  658.4'038

  ISBN 0-7153-9276-X

Typeset by Typesetters (Birmingham) Ltd
Smethwick, West Midlands
and printed in Great Britain
by Billing Limited, Worcester
for David & Charles Publishers plc
Brunel House Newton Abbot Devon

CONTENTS

To Marlies, Leah and Lani
– H.T.

To my parents, Jessie and Clifford Gill
– L.G.

In Britain there is still too strong a tendency to see presentation as something peripheral to an organisation's concerns. There are still too many company chairmen, other senior and middle executives, members of the professions and voluntary groups, who believe that, just because they do their jobs well, they can also communicate well. Harvey Thomas has devoted his professional life to showing such people the error of their ways and to assisting them in making an impact.

The cult of the amateur may have served Britain well in simpler times, but now professionalism is required of all of us in business and public life at all times. This is particularly true of presentation, as Harvey convincingly argues in this book.

Perhaps the suspicion too many people still harbour about effective use of public relations and other communications skills stems from their erroneous belief that good presentation can be used to mask a weak message. That isn't possible. What is all too possible is for a good message to go unheard because it isn't well presented.

I can think of no-one better qualified than Harvey Thomas to write a book about effective presentation.

Harvey Thomas' 'hands-on' experience of presentational issues ranges so widely that it can still surprise those who do not know him – from Billy Graham rallies to the Conservative Party Conference, from presenting his own television and radio programmes to advising senior businessmen on television and public speaking skills. Here he draws on this experience with all his customary enthusiasm for his subject. I am delighted that he has written this book which, I am confident, will convert many more people to the imperative of good presentation.

LORD YOUNG OF GRAFFHAM

Part One

PERSONALLY SPEAKING

1
NINETY-SEVEN COUNTRIES LATER

Experience is the name everyone
gives to his mistakes.

Oscar Wilde

It is the early hours of June 12, 1987, and I am standing on the first floor landing of Conservative Central Office, close to the Houses of Parliament. Most of the results of the General Election are in and it's already clear that Margaret Thatcher has won a remarkable victory. The atmosphere is electric. Outside, crowds are pressing against the barriers, bursting into song, waving flags and cheering, as one by one leading political figures and other VIPs make their way into the building.

Inside, the atmosphere is even more excited as at least 250 of us gather around the staircase or lean out of windows to watch the scene below. Hands are shaken, kisses exchanged, anecdotes swapped as the news we've all wanted to hear continues to pour out from television sets and teleprinters.

Now we are all waiting for the Prime Minister. For everyone involved from the newest volunteer to the senior professionals, it is a moment to savour, a time of undoubted triumph. Everyone is on a terrific high. Everyone, that is, but me! I *should* feel on top of the world. This is what I've worked eighteen hours a day for. This is what I've been down on my hands and knees for one minute, and teetering at the top of a step ladder the next. This is what has seen me lug milk crates into a muddy field to build an impromptu platform on a Wednesday and produce a high-tech laser show at Wembley on the Sunday. It's taken me on a 16,000 mile journey back and forth across Britain over the last four weeks. I've dealt with camera crews and school caretakers, checked out the latest technology and the village hall tap, met shop assistants and showbiz stars. I've run, walked, driven and flown and we've all done it to this end:

to win the hearts and minds of voters and give Mrs Thatcher an historic third term of government.

Why then, I ask myself, as I look at all the enthusiastic faces around me, do I feel so flat? I suppose a sense of anti-climax is inevitable to some degree after you achieve your objectives, but my despondency seems more than that. What I'm really asking myself is - just how necessary was my role of Presentation and Public Relations? Did my efforts make any difference? They'd surely have made it equally convincingly without me.

Later, when the party is over, I make my way slowly back down the staircase, retracing Mrs Thatcher's steps and out into the summer night. And as I do so I start remembering the little details of her arrival and triumphant progress through the building to Norman Tebbit's office, watched not just by her supporters here but by millions more on television. I recall how I'd put a particular extra light in here, another microphone there, so everyone could see and hear her; how I'd arranged for her to stop in a particular place for maximum visibility.

I remember how we'd seen to it that the barricades were placed, in consultation with the police, to ensure the crowds could see in reasonable comfort, how I'd opened the windows for her and the Party Chairman to lean out and wave to the people, even how I'd given out banners and ribbons, balloons and flags - that everyone was now waving wildly without any idea where they came from. And that was for just those few brief moments when the battle had been won. They'd been repeated by our teams a thousand-fold during the campaign itself and in the run up to it. By the time I reach my car my spirits have soared. My elation has come a little later than everyone else's, but it's there at last. My confidence is back.

By themselves all those tiny details might seem like silly little meaningless pieces: put them together and the jigsaw is complete. Miss one out and the whole picture can be flawed. Such detail is the key to successful communication and it applies whether you're organising a major conference or holding your AGM, whether you're making an after-dinner speech or appearing on TV.

This book is about Making an Impact - the 'drawing' of that overall picture and the details of planning and preparation and expertise that go into ensuring that things happen *because you want it that way*, rather than by chance. They are, if you like, the 'professional basics' from someone who's been in the business of presentation for over a quarter of a century.

I've been interested in communications, the medium and the message, ever since I heard Billy Graham preach at Haringey Arena in 1954 when I was fifteen. I was amazed at the way in which one man could capture and hold not just the attention of a vast audience but their hearts as well. It must have been something about the appeal of communications that pushed me towards both the law and the stage. Though I was articled to a solicitor for three years I was always more attracted to the idea of being a barrister, but the cost put it out of the question. I auditioned for the Royal Academy of Dramatic Art - RADA - in 1960 (like my brother Gareth who is now a successful - and very good - actor), but by the time my acceptance came through I'd already found a job I could commit myself to, and I turned the place down.

I'd met Maurice Rowlandson, one of Billy Graham's team, through my church youth fellowship and he told me the team were looking for someone to organise the land-line sound relays out of Manchester's Maine Road Stadium for the 1961 Crusade. This was a massive operation involving connections to 400 centres, each with a minimum of three churches working together. I jumped at the chance. For years I had dreamed of going to America - I'd pored over the Manhattan map so long I could have walked the streets of New York without a guide – (I still can) - and I asked the Billy Graham Association to give me a job in the States so that I could work my way through Bible College in Minneapolis.

It came as a bit of a shock to my middle class family who'd struggled to put me through Westminster School, but my mother gamely lent me £150 and I took the boat to New York City.

It was the start of a life that over the next twenty-five years was to take me into ninety-seven different countries and around the world many times. A career with people - famous and powerful, film stars and presidents and most of all 'volunteers'. The beginning was humble. I worked nights hauling mailbags for the Billy Graham Office. That job taught me a valuable lesson: never be afraid to get your hands dirty. People sometimes claim that my business simply involves thinking, being 'creative' and somehow waving the wand! One of the reasons for any success I've had is that I've always been ready to lift and carry, push chairs into position, fix something with a screwdriver and crawl under the stage (or nervously up the scaffolding)!

I still smile to myself when I'm advising clients on how to deal with the Press and I remember how my second press officer assignment for Billy Graham involved - literally - putting my shoulder to the press platform. It was a sort of scaffolding-on-wheels, and I manoeuvred it from place to place during the Los Angeles Crusade in 1963. Over 134,000 people crowded into the Coliseum for our final meeting - considerably more than the 90,000 who saw the Olympics there twenty-one years later. I went on to work for Graham's radio station, KAIM in Hawaii, where I hosted a seven-hour live-shift and, among other things, interviewed Martin Luther King and broadcast the announcement that President Kennedy had been assassinated. It was in Honolulu too that I began my work in television - hosting and interviewing.

I passed through Britain from time to time - I assisted Bill Brown, the director of the Earls Court Crusade in 1966, the year Cliff Richard made the first public declaration of his faith. I worked in Europe and all the other continents to arrange rallies, conferences and campaigns on a massive scale - always involving the motivating of volunteers, organisation, public relations and presentation.

Eventually, in 1977, I felt that I should return to my home country. I was becoming increasingly concerned about its decline, something one seemed to notice more abroad than at home. I was finding as I travelled from place to place that people were laughing at my British passport and making sarcastic remarks about the old country not being what she was. I had never been here long enough to vote but I knew instinctively that I was a Conservative.

In 1978 I returned and offered my skills - temporarily - as a consultant to the Party. A small honorarium was found 'to try out a few things' and I developed some special recruitment campaigns in various constituencies. When the 1979 election was called, I asked to be introduced to the person who set up and organised their conferences and rallies. 'What do you mean "set-up"?' I was asked. 'Well,' I said, 'who co-ordinates the presentation, liaises with the media, sets up the stage, the sound, the lights, speech rehearsals, all the TV arrangements?' 'Oh,' I was told, 'there's always someone who puts out a microphone'! 'Right,' I said, 'lead me to it.' And that's how our relationship, which has seen three general elections, ten annual conferences, many by-elections, campaigns, rallies, meetings, speeches, broadcasts and special events, began.

In the political side of my work, the task has been to deal with all aspects of audio-visual presentation and to help politicians and others to make the best use of their skills on television and radio or in their constituency.

It hasn't always been easy. Sometimes the simplest practical aids have caused deep suspicion and even downright hostility. In 1982 I introduced an electronic adjustable-height lectern for conferences - something that I had used for years. The lectern can go down to table-top height when the platform guests are listening to the debate, thus giving them a clear view of the speaker and the audience, and the audience a clear view of them. It can then go up to the right level for each speaker. Sounds simple? It took me three years to convince different politicians to use this 'monster'. One even told me it would 'frighten the whole Cabinet, leaping up and down like that'. (Collectors of trivia might like to know that Mrs Thatcher has the lectern set at a height of 99 centimetres).

Michael Caine said in a television interview at the end of 1988 that when he was going to address RADA students they were told by the tutors: 'Listen to *what* he says - but not *how* he says it.' Impossible! How you say it adds 90 per cent of the *impact* to your message.

There is still a feeling in this country that mastering personal communication skills, employing technique and technology to give your message impact is somehow cheating - not playing fair. They argue that if you've got a good message it will somehow get itself across. Most of the time that is rubbish.

Effective communication *impact* throughout history has depended on *how* something is presented far more than *what* it is. If you can't be heard, you can't be understood. There is no moral or ethical contradiction in giving your message maximum impact. If what you want to say is true, saying it well to as wide an audience as possible won't affect that truth. I worked for Billy Graham for fifteen years and our only concern throughout that time was to get more and more people to make a personal Christian commitment, using whatever honest means we could. This book is certainly about pushing yourself or your organisation forward but it's not about treading on others. Moreover, if your message is rubbish, lots of polish may make it sparkle, but it won't give it impact.

I draw the comparison with a slide show. A good public relations man can focus the projector, set it the right distance from the screen, turn down the lights, and play the right music, but he cannot project a slide that is not in the projector. Presentation and public relations is projection and focus rather than false 'image'.

I've never been able to 'sell' anything I didn't believe in, a fact I discovered early in my working life. When I was living in Hawaii doing the early morning radio show I needed to make some more money, so in the afternoons I became a salesman, selling pictures of babies! The idea was to scan the local paper for recent births and then turn up at the family home to persuade the proud new mother to commit herself to an album to be taken over the next two years and to pay $200 for the service. That was an awful lot of money in 1963, especially when they could so easily do the job themselves. I made a poor salesman because my heart wasn't in it, and I soon quit. On the other hand, when I *do* believe in something I can pull out all the stops.

Although much of my experience was gained in the United

States or from Americans you won't find this book a eulogy on American methods - but over there they do start from a different position. *They* ask: 'What is our goal and how are we going to achieve it?' In this country *we* ask: 'How do we usually do things?' I was once being interviewed on the BBC's *Today* programme and Brian Redhead asked me, 'Don't you feel all this stage management is phony? Isn't the image hiding the politics?' I turned my head away from the microphone and spoke to the studio wall. 'No, Brian,' I said, 'it's a way of presenting things properly.' He said, 'Harvey, would you turn towards the microphone please. Our listeners can't hear you.' I made my point.

We must get away from this notion of 'gentlemen and players' which so bedevils British life. We are superb losers (how we all cheered Eddie Edwards in the Calgary Olympics) but we can't quite get used to the idea of winning, even less the idea of planning and organising and working to win. We seem to think that if it doesn't just 'happen', it's unfairly done. This attitude is ridiculous. You and your client should aim at being number one: the goal is to produce the best. Remember too that you cannot afford to ignore presentation know-how for long. If you don't learn it, your opponents will. If not today, then certainly tomorrow morning!

The results of presentation and public relations are sometimes measurable - an election result here, a sales figure there - but frequently the effect is intangible.

Why, for instance, has Glasgow, for so long derided as drab and dreadful, now acquired an exciting, cultured image, whereas Edinburgh, once the Athens of the North, is now increasingly associated with AIDS and junkies? Why do yuppies find it smart to shop at Marks and Spencer but not at Woolworth - they both started as penny bazaars. One could give example after example with dozens of factors affecting the image of an individual or the identity of a corporation. What matters is to realise that such images are not conjured out of thin air, they are built by hundreds of tiny bricks painstakingly assembled by someone who knows what the finished picture should look like. Before I go on to show you the bricks - or the jigsaw pieces - let me first give you a couple of examples of good and bad public relations that happened to me.

In October 1984, during the Conservative Conference in Brighton, the IRA blew up the Grand Hotel in an attempt to murder the Prime Minister and the Cabinet. The bomb was in the room directly below mine. I was three metres above the centre of the explosion. It went off at 2.45am as I slept, dreaming of my wife, Marlies, and the birth of our first baby (Leah) due any day. The force of the blast hurled me into the air, shooting me and the ceiling of my room up an entire floor. In seconds I was falling again, masonry and timber bouncing off me and around me as I covered my mouth and nose with my hands. I thumped to a stop, three floors down, lying across a girder that was sticking out over a five storey drop. Ten tons of rubble were lying on top of me. My eyes were closed by the rubble and I couldn't move an inch. I *knew* I was going to die.

It took two and a half hours for a team of skilled and brave firemen to reach me, inching their way through the danger and debris and risking their lives to save mine. Astonishingly, I was basically unharmed so I was able to spend the time concentrating on breathing (I had only a small pocket of trapped air), praying and thinking, and finally chatting to the firemen as they got nearer and nearer. I was helped by my not insubstantial eighteen-stone, six-foot-four-inch frame and by the fact that I neither smoke nor drink so that, though the explosion happened while I was asleep, I was alert immediately. With lungs strong enough to resist the blast, I escaped with cuts and bruises - and two small stones embedded in my right ear system which suddenly emerged two weeks later during a flight to Canada; the air pressure must have worked them loose. Others of course were not so fortunate. That bomb killed five people and badly injured others, some permanently.

I felt no lasting shock effects either at the time or since and I feel no personal hatred towards the terrorists. The Bible teaches Christians to forgive - and if Christian believers were more effective communicators there would be fewer criminals. As I lay under the rubble I learnt much about myself, my faith and human nature.

A few weeks afterwards I got a bill for my stay from the Grand Hotel - including the full charge for the night my room disintegrated! I hasten to add that there's a new team there now!

But if that's how *not* to conduct your public relations, here's the opposite example.

In the late sixties I was in Australia flying on Ansett Airlines from Darwin to Brisbane across 2,000 miles of outback with one stop at the small mining town of Mt Isa. On the first leg of the journey I realised something was wrong with the third engine - I had flown enough by then to sense trouble. We made an emergency landing at Mt Isa where the plane was fixed via telephone instructions from Brisbane. There actually was one chap holding onto the phone and shouting to his colleague at the back of the Boeing 727 engine, 'Can you see a nut marked A?' 'Yes.' 'Then turn it three times to the left.'

No wonder we were feeling apprehensive as we got back on board, but our attention was soon diverted by a spectacular electric storm in the distance. As we watched the black clouds churn and the jagged lightning leap across the sky, the pilot's voice came on the intercom.

'Good afternoon, ladies and gentlemen. I'm sure you're all admiring the storm and it's quite a show, but I think I ought to tell you that Brisbane's on the other side of it.' He paused to let that sink in and then continued: 'I want you to imagine a cork in a bucket of water. Now you can do anything to that cork, push it under, flick it up, put it on its side, or make it somersault, but it will always float back to the surface unharmed.' Another pause. 'Now, ladies and gentlemen, that's what this plane is like. This plane will do anything in that storm, we may even turn over or do a somersault but it won't do the plane any harm. I've got two computers up here.' Someone said, 'What about us?' and the captain went on: 'Oh yes, and two other pilots as well so we'll be through the storm in about five minutes. What I want you to do is strap yourselves in, hang on tight and we'll just go through.' We all strapped ourselves in and he said: 'Right, are you ready?' There was no reply so he asked again: 'I can't hear you, are you ready?' 'Yes' came the tentative response and he put the plane into a sweeping arc and with deliberate drama turned right into the storm.

He was right. We bounced up, we dropped down, we tossed and bumped and flipped so much that the luggage in the overhead racks slid across the ceiling. But we came through and nobody was ill and nobody panicked.

It was that extraordinary experience that made me realise the power of public relations. The pilot had presented his case so well that everyone had understood what was happening and *had been able to deal with it.* How different things might have been if he'd said nothing or just - as many do - 'Please return to your seats and fasten your belts immediately'.

That pilot knew his business. But such skills don't come easily to most of us. By the end of this book I hope you will at least know how to learn them.

2
UNACCUSTOMED AS I AM

Curtsey while you're thinking what to say. It saves time.
Lewis Carroll

The last few years have seen an explosion in the number of public speaking opportunities, and the demand is going to keep on growing through the nineties.

At one time, apart from the odd toast or brief vote of thanks, most people could go through life safe in the knowledge that they'd never have to get to their feet and address an audience. No more! As we approach the 1990s, men and women are becoming more informed and more involved. Privatisation means thousands more shareholders who want a say at their Annual General Meeting. More parents want to determine how their children's schools are run. More trade union members want a voice in local meetings at grass roots level.

People are becoming interested in community politics and local pressure groups. Middle and senior managers are now expected to speak at meetings or, worse, to make important presentations or sales pitches on their company's behalf.

At the beginning of 1989, direct broadcast satellites began to beam multiple channels onto British television sets and most American cities have dozens to choose from. The demand has come for new and varied spokesmen to interview, and the speed and intimacy of news gathering nowadays means that anyone can be catapulted into the limelight as a witness to or representative of a newsworthy event.

It's estimated in America that more than 31 million people go to over 325,000 conferences and conventions every year, and now the trend is accelerating on this side of the Atlantic. That's just one kind of occasion where you might need to speak. Huge numbers of people who would have been hidden from public view in the eighties can expect to be asked to speak in public in the nineties. Company executives, club secretaries, athletes, shop stewards, parents, local government officials - the list may not be exactly endless but it's growing so fast that you are likely to find yourself on it sooner or later.

The 'regular' speakers too - clergymen, lecturers and others - are finding that their audiences now demand a better presentation of the message. They are no longer prepared to be bored by a meaningless monotone mouthing of words which might have been vital if only they had been presented well. And the boom in technology means that you can no longer count on your little speech being made in some obscure location with only fifty people to listen to it. Someone will undoubtedly be making a tape recording or catching you on video.

Yet, fear of public speaking remains one of the commonest phobias. Most people would rather walk across hot coals. The mere thought of it can be enough to make a victim start sweating and shaking.

There is, of course, no need to feel terrified - or even mildly afraid! Really! With practice and commitment almost anyone can be a good public speaker. I've seen people change dramatically both their attitude and their ability in just one three-hour tuition session.

On the other hand, there are a lot of people in prominent positions who give speeches regularly, who send their audiences into dreamy hypnosis with no effort at all, simply because they haven't learned the basics. As I have developed my public speaking and personal presentation training I have been staggered to realise the extent of the inability to speak or present a case effectively by leaders in every section of life and from all around the world. *You* could do better!

Practice makes perfect

The secret of successful public speaking - as with most other skills - is preparation and practice, practice, practice. Woody Allen tells of the man who had to abandon his dreams of being the world's greatest violin player when he realised it involved learning to play the violin.

Before you stand up, know your objective, know your subject, know your audience.

There are no short cuts. The best speakers can make it look easy, but they've probably been in serious training on video or at least in front of a full length mirror for hours on end. As you draft your speech, keep the communication order in mind: *interest* first, *inform* second, *involve* third. You will not make an impact unless you catch the interest of your audience *first* - and hold it.

Then rehearse!

The most 'spontaneous' speeches are frequently the most rehearsed. Winston Churchill, a man with a few oratory skills, was overheard muttering to himself as he strolled around the garden in Downing Street: 'I had not intended to say *this* to the House today, I had *not* intended to say this to the House today, I had not intended to say this to the House *today* . . .'

There is, of course, a danger in rehearsing too much. I had a friend in my youth group, called Paul, who was desperate to be in the church play. He begged, he pleaded and, in the end, managed to convince the director that he could do it. He was given a part - with two words: 'I did'. It was the answer to a question and Paul rehearsed this line as if he were playing Hamlet at the National. He said it in different accents, he said it loud, he said it soft, he said it so often around us that we were all sick of these two monotonous words.

The big night came and his moment arrived. We all held our breath - and out came: 'Did I?'

Poor Paul. It was a salutary lesson on the dangers of over-rehearsing which has stayed with me. Paul, by the way, is today a good and successful actor and still a friend.

Know your subject

Public speaking is *not* 'parrotting'. That can get you into terrible trouble. A family invited the vicar to dinner. Although they did not normally say 'grace', the hostess thought she should put on a show for the clergyman's benefit. So, as they sat down to eat, she asked her daughter: 'Please say grace, darling', desperately hoping that the girl had learnt something at school.

'Darling' looked blank. 'What shall I say?' she asked. 'Just,' said her mother through gritted teeth, 'say what you've heard Mummy say.'

The girl nodded, bowed her head and said, 'Oh God, why did the vicar have to come on a Friday?'

The point I'm making is that you must know your *content* thoroughly. Not just memorise it, but be completely familiar with the subject, the arguments and the overall thrust of your speech. If you *know* your subject, you can develop confidence, calm your nerves, and make the odd deviation without losing your thread. That confidence - and practice - allows you to concentrate on the other elements of successful speech-making which I'll come to later.

If you're struggling desperately simply to remember your theme, you've got no chance to deal with anything else. The words - the content - of your speech are obviously the basis of it, but they only account for something like ten per cent of the impact on your listeners. The other ninety per cent is presentation - body language, eye contact, tone, speed, attitude to the audience, confidence and clarity.

In a big international committee meeting in Copenhagen Billy Graham was in the chair with his associate Walter Smyth behind him. I saw Billy speak to a local steward who went out to return a few minutes later with a bunch of pictures of Walter Smyth, which he handed around the table. When the surprise became obvious, Billy apologised for his strong North Carolina accent and explained that he had actually asked for 'pitchers of water' *not* 'pictures of Walter'. Speak clearly!

Knowing your subject means research beforehand. I speak regularly at the International Media Conference of the Hanns Seidel Foundation, the political education wing of the Bavarian Conservative Party, in Germany. For the 1988 Budapest conference my topic was 'Helsinki and Afterwards - the Role of the Media in International Relations'. Now, I was (fairly) confi-

---

SPARKLING UNDERSTANDING

At a committee meeting in Paris in the sixties Billy Graham tasted sparkling mineral water, apparently for the first time. 'Say, this is good stuff,' he said, 'I wish we could have this at every crusade!'

Somebody - I never found out who - took Billy literally. For years shipments of sparkling French mineral water would arrive mysteriously at crusades around the world - just before Billy did.

Unfortunately you needed a bottle opener to get the top off, so Billy never could drink it on the platform after all. However, as his original remark had merely been a passing comment, he happily drank ordinary water and we never mentioned the shipments at all.

---

dent that I could deal with the second half of that theme - it's my speciality. But I had to swot up on the Helsinki Agreement on Human Rights before I even drafted my speech. I certainly didn't want any slip-ups in front of an audience which would contain experts in the field. (As it happens, I got salmonella poisoning two days beforehand and had to cancel my trip!)

Who are you talking to?

As well as knowing your content you must also know your *audience*.

A man from the Welsh valleys died and went to Heaven. St Peter welcomed him and said, 'Tell our gathered multitudes something interesting that happened to you in your life. What will it be?' The man thought for a moment and then said excitedly, 'I'll tell them about the flood we had down our valley when the river overflowed and we had to use buckets to bale out the cellar.' 'That sounds fascinating,' said St Peter politely, 'but I ought to tell you that Noah is in the audience!'

You need to know basic facts about your audience: its size, whether one sex predominates, political or other leanings, what brings these people together and whether they're strangers or friends to each other. You will want to know if you're the only speaker or, if you're one of several, at which point in the programme you will make your contribution. All this, of course, will be either self-evident or obtainable from the organisers.

But you can do a bit of on-the-spot research yourself. In the theatre it's 'not done' to peep through the curtains at an audience, but I like either to get a look at them beforehand or at least at the room where I'll be speaking.

Usually, when you are invited to speak, the organisers put you in a 'green room' or hospitality suite and then whisk you on to the platform at the last minute. I always find some point where I can pop into the room or church or auditorium. That way I can check the sound system and the lighting and have a look at the seating. The chairs may be arranged in undisturbed neat rows or they may have been moved and turned for discussion groups. If it's the latter, you may find that people have been talking to their colleagues or friends during a previous speaker or moving around the room. You know that you may have to work a bit harder to hold their attention.

If you can't find out much about your audience beforehand, then you have to do it at the beginning of your speech. Your opening is not just your introduction to the subject, but also the introduction between you and your listeners.

I recently spoke to a group of international religious broadcasters. My aim was to encourage and motivate them to develop religious broadcasting across Europe. I did not know them, or their religious leanings or even whether they would be familiar with various church leaders around the world. They obviously knew of *my* connection with the Conservative Party but I had no idea of *their* political leanings.

So, I opened with a true story of when I was preaching at a black church in Los Angeles in the mid-seventies. The church's pastor was a marvellous preacher who, years later, spent the first ten minutes of the opening prayer at the Republican National Convention in Dallas in 1984 telling the Lord how fortunate He was to have the Republican Party on His side. Every face in that church was black, except mine. After an hour or more of the service it was my turn to speak. I stood up - (at

6ft 4in I'm a lot taller than he was) - and he stood up. He put his arm up on my shoulder and announced to the congregation: 'Our brother Thomas. He may be white but his heart is black!'

Now, I told that story to break the ice and to note audience reactions. I learned that many of them knew the pastor (I could see them nodding when I mentioned his name) and that meant they were likely to know some of the other people I was planning to refer to. They had smiled and even laughed, so I knew that whatever their political views, they were not antagonistic towards me. They were warm and responsive to humour and a light touch.

If their reaction had been different, if they'd been too serious or looked blank or even disapproving, *then* I would have continued in a different vein. I would have learned from my introduction that they wanted a less anecdotal approach and a heavier, more 'theological' one. That's what I mean about the need to discover, very quickly, what kind of an audience you have.

On that occasion my objective was to uplift and inspire the group. This is the third thing to bear in mind when planning a speech. Know your content, know your audience but, above all, know your *objective*. Ask yourself: what am I trying to do here? Do I want to inform, educate, inspire, persuade or just entertain? Knowing your objective determines the form, attitude and content of your speech.

Planning a speech

When it comes to planning what you're going to say, the key rule to remember is that the written word and the spoken word are completely different. What looks good on paper will probably be long-winded, over-complicated and boring. I've listened to hundreds of speeches where I could 'hear' every comma, bracket and italic.

Speak *out loud* what you've written - either on your own, into a tape or video recorder, or in front of family or friends. Listen to yourself. Watch yourself if you can and analyse as objectively as possible whether you are applying the basic principles, and whether your family or friends give the response you will want from your audience.

Make notes or draft an outline; highlight it where necessary or draw it up in the form of headlines, whichever method works best for you. And make sure it is *speech* not reading material! See that the content is accurate, the sections and argument clear and headlined, and the flow easy to follow.

The length of your speech will usually be someone else's decision. If it is yours, err on the side of brevity. It's amazing how many people confuse quality with quantity. There is nothing worse than a dreary bore who loves the sound of his or her own voice. At one conference a man in the audience tired of listening to such a speaker and left the room to go for a cup of coffee. On his return he found the same speaker still on his feet. As he slipped back into his seat the man whispered to his neighbour in dismay, 'I thought he would have finished by now.' The weary reply came back. 'He finished an hour ago but he won't stop.'

It is far harder to speak for three minutes than for thirty-three. Whatever the length, train yourself to edit ruthlessly. Chuck the waffle, the clichés and the jargon and keep it simple.

Don't try and say too much. Whether a speech is five minutes or forty-five, you can, realistically, only expect to impart a maximum of three points.

You may understand what you're saying - you'll hopefully have rehearsed it many times - but your audience only gets to hear it once. You have to get interest, understanding and response from just one delivery. There is no second chance. Plan it, rehearse it - but watch the audience to assess their reaction and be prepared to adjust your approach if their feedback tells you to.

Don't be like one speaker I heard of. A local journalist asked him what he was going to say. 'How do I know what I'm going to say until after I've heard what I said?' was the reply.

The natural approach

Once you're on your feet, be yourself. Be genuine. A false show requires an enormous amount of wasteful effort and phoneyness always shows through in the end. Even actors who are capable of playing many parts perform best in roles where they can project a lot of their own personality. It is said that John Wayne was once asked to read Shakespeare. He opened: 'To be or not to be - that is the . . . say, who wrote this stuff anyway?'

By all means, look to successful speakers for example and technique but don't try to copy any other person. You are an exclusive - an original - but you can only be a cheap copy of someone else. When I'm training someone I never try to change his or her personality. I try to draw it out so that the inner feelings for the subject are on show. A good speech is not just words. It is emotion, passion, conviction - even for statistics.

Don't try too hard to change your voice; every kind of accent is heard and accepted nowadays. But do use it to its maximum potential. Vary your tone, speed and volume. Get the emphasis right.

A microphone is *always* an asset, not because you wouldn't be heard without one (you probably would in most cases) but because it gives you 'presence' and authority as you speak. A mike can also be used for special effects. I sometimes demonstrate this by the 'personal whisper'. I pick someone near the back of the room, speak quietly close to the mike and have a pleasant chat that excludes everybody else in the audience.

Use your body language to bring the audience with you. Your facial anticipation will help them to laugh at your punch line. Humour, used properly, is not the enemy of gravitas.

I'll talk more about technical things in another chapter but a speaker has all kinds of audio-visual aids at his disposal - slides, charts, diagrams, video, film and so on. By all means use them to lend interest or explanation to what you're saying or to make a fuller presentation, but *don't make them a substitute for your content or performance.* All your presentation must point towards the message - your content.

Use gestures if they come naturally to you but make sure they can be seen - they often get hidden behind the podium – and slide your notes across the lectern rather than turning them over; that is a distraction.

Use humour and anecdotes but be sure they illustrate a point, and be informal whenever you can. Don't patronise or lecture your audience, but you can assume your own authority. 'I think that', 'in my opinion', 'it is my belief' . . . all weaken your content by defensiveness. You can usually cross these phrases out.

RING OF CONFIDENCE

George Bush now projects confidence both in his speeches and his television appearances. In early 1989, though, Vice-President Dan Quayle appears to have had his confidence destroyed by the press and media attacks on him. I think he *has* the potential to grow into the job, but it's going to take time.

At a conference in Washington soon after the inauguration his gestures were artificial and his delivery stilted and un-natural. Even his attempt to wave at the 4,000 delegates was a failure: he kept his elbow tucked into his waist and failed to raise his hand up high. It looked weak and was a vivid demonstration of his lack of confidence in himself.

His reading of the speech itself showed the same attitude and over-emphasised his efforts to impress the audience by the intellectual content alone. A pity.

I hope he is given a fair chance to get some faith back in himself.

Getting a reaction

Never speak for more than four, or at most five, minutes without making your audience *do* something. They may laugh, applaud, look at their neighbours, raise their hands, whatever. In the business these spots are known as 'clap lines' and they are a vital part of holding an audience's attention. In the 1990s an average attention span is likely to be about three minutes. Although your listeners usually want you to succeed, they don't owe you anything; you have to *win* their attention, their response, their conversion.

Sometimes you have to work pretty hard for all this. The Prime Minister did at the 1982 Information Technology Year Conference at the Barbican. In a planning blunder she had been given the opening session of the first day, so that she was faced at nine in the morning with a cold audience of strangers. It immediately became clear she was going to have to do something to draw them out and five minutes into her speech she diverted from the text and mentioned the names of two men on the platform who had won an award. 'These men have done a fantastic job for Britain,' she said, 'and I think they deserve a round of applause, don't you?'

She turned towards them and clapped. The audience followed suit and the simple device did the trick. The ice was broken. What's more, the audience realised what she had done. They laughed with her and gave her more applause to continue. That kind of thinking on your feet is hard for the novice but it's an important element of an effective speech.

As you talk you must constantly be asking yourself 'Am I achieving my object or taking the right steps towards achieving it?' If you are, great, carry on. If not, you need to be able to assess *why* not and to change your presentational tack, if not your content.

So, if you've been humorous but they've remained serious, then switch quietly and confidently into a more serious vein. For this you need feedback and that means eye contact. Don't just stare at one person, range over a wide group of people. The principle is the same whether you're talking to ten or to ten thousand - let them know you are talking to each one personally.

Even if you're faced with bright lights you can still look out and feel reaction. You can see movement, you can hear indrawn breath, you can hear laughter and applause. What is drawing these reactions is the audience thinking that *you* are looking at *them*. This does not mean, of course, that you cannot consult your notes or other cues. Here, the rule is - as it is with television appearances - you get away with anything so long as your audience believes it is deliberate. They will only be embarrassed if *you* are.

Give your audience time to react. Don't 'step on a laugh', as they say in the theatre, by pressing on too fast. People tend to speak faster when they stand up to give a speech. In fact, if you're obeying the rules you will speak more slowly. So, for a speech of ten minutes plan your outline to occupy two-thirds of that time, for fifteen minutes to an hour plan for three-quarters.

One famous writer was asked if he thought a play should have a beginning, a middle and an end. 'Yes, of course,' he said, 'but not necessarily in that order.' I tend to a more traditional view myself or as the preacher said, 'Tell 'em what you're going to say, say it and tell 'em you've said it.'

It really does take people three goes to absorb something. So your introduction will, as well as introducing you and the audience to each other, also introduce your theme. Show people where you are going or they won't go with you. Headline each section so that the audience can see the next step and follow you easily.

The bulk of your speech is the meat of it, the heart of what you want to say. Remember your theme and concentrate on putting across one point at a time, using the devices I mentioned earlier. By all means repeat points - on purpose - to reinforce your message. Don't be repetitious by accident, that's boring.

The same principle applies to public speaking as it does to television discussion. Aim to win the person, not just the argument. You should plan your conclusion that way, to get the response you want. Sum up clearly and strongly and hopefully draw the natural applause which will enable you to sit down. You can always use a good pay-off line - one which will draw applause or laughter in its own right - during which you sit down and the applause increases.

Visual and other aids

If you use any visual aids, remember that they are *aids* not crutches. Try not to turn around to look at slides. They should merely be a back-up for your speech. In recent years, too many speakers have begun to use slides as their prompts or even their scripts. Nothing can substitute for the personal presentation and visual aids are there solely to reinforce the clarity of the content.

One or two final pointers. Never touch any alcohol before making a speech. You need a clear head. Sparkling mineral water is the best drink for a public speaker to sip. It won't make you burp unless you take huge gulps (with the exception of one or two very gassy ones). Ordinary flat water can give you indigestion. Iced water constricts the throat. Ashbourne is a wide favourite among my clients.

If you suddenly get tongue-tied in a sentence and mix something up, smile at yourself (the most endearing trait of all to an audience) and say something on the lines of 'There must have been something in that coffee' and then start the sentence again slowly and deliberately. The audience will be in sympathy with you and no-one will mind at all about the slip-up. In fact, one of the most comforting things to remember about public speaking is that audience sympathy is virtually always with you when you start. They actually want to hear what you've got to say so you start off with a major advantage.

Try to record each speech so that you can play it back and learn from your mistakes or your successes. Listen to it as objectively as you can. Take the trouble to make an honest assessment of yourself.

Finally, every good public speaker has had to start somewhere. It may be a good idea not even to wait to be asked. Start speaking up at meetings or other suitable occasions. Force yourself to say something even if it's only 'I agree'. That way you gain confidence and experience. You'd be amazed at the number of curriculum vitae I see with 'Speaker at Conservative Party Conference'. It looks impressive experience but all it means is that they have managed to get called from the floor

PUBLIC SPEAKING

The secret is practice, analysis and more practice!

1 Know your objective - convert, inform, persuade, inspire, entertain?
2 Know your subject *and* your content. Don't parrot or rely on reading the script. The content wins their minds, your presentation wins their hearts.
3 Know the audience - or find out about them through your opening comments.
4 Know your presentation - slides, video, etc and rehearse it.
5 Keep it simple. Headline your sections. Let the theme or message 'flow' easily.
6 'Read' your audience's feed-back, monitor your progress.
7 Don't be phoney, you will look and sound like a pompous twit.
8 **Format**
   a) The *introduction* is to open the communication between you, the members of your audience and probably your subject.
   b) The *meat* is what you want to say, preferably in two or three points.
   c) The *conclusion* is a summary review to lead the audience towards the objective of your speech.
9 **Presentation**
   a) Prepare the room, equipment and your appearance.
   b) Watch the people in your audience. Make them respond or react at least every 3-4 minutes.
   c) Use anecdotes or humour, relevant to the speech.
   d) Let your body speak but keep control of it. Use facial expression.
   e) Anything is acceptable if your audience believes you are doing it deliberately.
   f) Vary your speed and the tone of your voice.
   g) Speak clearly.
   h) When you have finished, shut-up and sit down!
10 **Microphones**
   a) *Always* have a PA system if you can, even for thirty people. It's not volume, it's 'presence'.
   b) Keep your voice moving in the direction of the micro-phone.
   c) Use a microphone for 'special effects' (a whisper close to a mike can be very effective).
11 Is what you have to say *interesting?*

to give a three-minute contribution in a debate.

Start and soon you'll be hard to stop. But be careful. A politician got home late at the end of a day's campaigning, with his wife beside him. As he flopped into his chair he said, 'Boy, I'm exhausted. Do you realise I had to make eight speeches today?'

'*You're* exhausted?' said his wife. 'I had to listen to them!'

3
GETTING ON THE RIGHT WAVELENGTH

Never make a defence or apology before
you be accused.   *King Charles I*

Reality is television

C.P. Scott, legendary editor of the *Manchester Guardian*, is said
to have remarked when he heard about a new-fangled invention
called television, 'Television? The word is half Latin and half
Greek. No good can come of it.' Decades later, some people,
particularly politicians and corporate chiefs, seem to view it
with the same suspicion.

Television is a reality of modern life. Ninety-eight per cent
of homes have one or more sets; most people watch three or
four hours every day. Millions get their first impressions of a
person or an event from it. Newspapers and magazines now
expand and elaborate on the news rather than break it. For
those who read little, television is often their only source of
information.

So, the modern communicator has to master this medium,
which is going to grow even more powerful in the next few
years. Cable and satellite television have put twenty or more
channels on our screens. And as television expands, your
chances of appearing on it grow accordingly greater.

Andy Warhol said: 'In the future everyone will be famous
for fifteen minutes'. For once he was prophetic. Television will
need you! More programmes, more channels, longer viewing
hours, mean that it has a greedy appetite for experts, com-
mentators and people with stories to tell, opinions to express,
knowledge to pass on.

No more than ten per cent of non-professionals have ever

had training, but you *can* still present yourself or your company well.

There are all kinds of circumstances in which you might find yourself on TV: a one-to-one interview in the studio or in the street, as a member of a panel or participating audience, a contributor to a debate or as an eye-witness to events. A huge number of middle and senior managers are now finding themselves, all of a sudden, company spokesmen on radio or television - frequently on network as well as regional. In many cases, the reason is a problem and that one appearance can either minimise the damage to the company, or destroy the organisation in a few seconds.

After the British Midland Boeing air crash in January 1989, the BM Chairman, Michael Bishop, handled the public relations extremely well. He was fully available for television and radio interviews from minutes after the crash. He was obviously upset but he had all the available facts at his fingertips; he was clearly on top of both the rescue operation and the investigation, but it was equally obvious that his first concern was looking after the injured and the relatives of those who had died.

As a damage limitation exercise it was superb. It was interesting too that the impact of the 'third-person' reports on TV was strong here. Mr Bishop didn't say too much about the care that BM was taking of relatives and injured people, he just made the information fully available to the news media who reported, almost on his behalf, the considerable lengths the airline was going to in giving help. On television he was quiet, authoritative, genuine and articulate.

One of the first points that I stress in my TV training is that television is a *visual* medium! Sounds obvious, doesn't it? But it's remarkable how many people forget or never even consider that essential element. On television your appearance, and by that I mean everything from facial expression through clothes to body language - your whole attitude in fact - will make a bigger impression than anything you actually say. Viewers will not recall the finer points of Mike Bishop's, Mrs Thatcher's or Neil Kinnock's comments, but they *will* remember the manner, the attitude, the tone and the way they were put across.

Television is an immensely personal medium so another key factor is naturalness, or perhaps a slightly exaggerated naturalness. Be yourself on television; be genuine. If you are telling lies or trying to be something you are not, television will show you up. Sooner or later phonies are exposed. You may have idols and heroes whom you would love to be like, but slick smoothness is rarely what's needed.

This has changed as people have come to know television over the last twenty years. We are, perhaps subconsciously, aware of what we see. If Lord Home, formerly Alec Douglas-Home, is on television today, we recognise him for what he *is* - a warm person and a straightforward politician and statesman. Twenty years ago a less TV-orientated society wanted to see a slick polished 'show'. Lord Home lost the election partially because of this attitude.

So don't 'perform'. Performance is for actors in a theatre. As soon as you start to put on an act you're in trouble. If you have something to hide or nothing to say, avoid going on television and proving it in public.

Assuming, however, that you do have something worth saying, gut-level genuineness will help to make you a success. The most memorable television personalities are those who have the ability to be natural - real - on camera. President Reagan was a master of it, which is why, in good or bad times politically, there remained an enormous personal affection for him from the people of America. He won the *people*, even if he didn't always win the argument.

Reagan always obeyed the rules - don't try and blind viewers with a heavy intellectual speech if you are not a heavy intellectual (and don't bore them with one if you are). Talk as one human being to another. In the mid-eighties Reagan had to make a speech on television explaining the new tax reforms to convince people that they were necessary. Not the most exciting or riveting subject in the world and a political minefield. He spent eighteen minutes of a twenty-minute appearance talking to the people on the themes of 'the need to make things right between us . . . a fairer deal for Americans . . . sort out the things that are wrong . . . ' He only spent two minutes saying - in simple outline - what the tax plans actually were.

When the Democrat came on to reply, he started off: 'I have to agree with nearly all the President has said . . .' President Reagan won the hearts first, then took the people along with him through an argument in such simple terms that anybody disagreeing looked argumentative and petty.

Reagan, of course, made it look easy. That's a real talent and not everyone can possess it to that extent. But we can all make a great deal more of what we are.

Still, the *substance* has to be there and the *presentation* needs to be rehearsed. My clients have to have substance, in commerce and industry, religion and politics, or I cannot do anything with them. If they win thirty seconds on prime-time television they have, in effect, been given £50,000 of advertising. For that they should be ready to prepare and rehearse.

The classic in bad television was performed by the Labour candidate in the 1988 Govan by-election. In a televised debate he was completely unprepared and had to admit on camera that he really didn't understand the subject that he was discussing.

When you're invited

Before you accept an invitation to go on television, find out everything you can about the programme. What is the subject, who is the interviewer, who else is taking part, will it be live or recorded, are the viewers regional, national, general, specialist? Will your interview be edited and what will the final length of your contribution be?

All that helps you to prepare and influences your decision whether or not to accept. It's not always to your advantage to go on television: you may be unfamiliar with or unsure of the subject, you may not wish to appear with certain people, and I'm not necessarily talking about your opponents. For instance, I'd be delighted to appear with Arthur

BIG ON THE BOX

Here are some of the people I think present themselves particularly well on television. I'm reluctant to name any poor performers because they may improve in time.

The two Kenneths: Baker and Clarke. They are completely different types physically: Clarke is warm and bubbly; Baker seems more polished but conveys the human touch. Both are relaxed and comfortable with their subjects.

Virginia Bottomley has a gentle approach and is very good at being herself.

Labour's John Smith comes across well as a tough, sharp thinking person with a hint of softness somewhere.

Bryan Gould handled being Labour's front man in the last general election reasonably well. A bit too smooth sometimes, particularly when having difficulty with his answer.

David Blunkett does well in spite of the natural sympathy we have for his blindness. By that I mean he manages to put it aside and project himself over it.

Denis Healey is good as long as he is not angry. Often politicians are more effective on a chat show than in a political programme. Healey demonstrated this on *This is Your Life*.

David Steel is quite good and natural. He comes across particularly well 'down the line' because he's able to chat easily to camera.

David Owen usually gives a good performance but one can always see a hardness coming through.

Lord Thorneycroft is superb, a natural: warm, humorous and effective.

Curiously, many actors find it hard to play themselves. Michael Caine is an exception, both controlled and natural, as are Judi Dench and her husband Michael Williams.

A lot of businessmen could do with help. One who has mastered the medium is Sir John Harvey Jones who manages to come over not as a big businessman but as an ordinary human being talking common sense.

Most preachers are awful on television: how often has *Songs of Praise* been ruined by the pompous clergyman at the end. One of the best is the Rev Lord Donald Soper, former head of the Methodists, who is particularly powerful on television. He has, of course, never hidden behind his pulpit but been out perfecting his communication skills with the people at Speakers' Corner. Cardinal Hume, despite the formality of his religion, brings in a calm and relaxed touch.

Scargill because my personal, softly, softly approach would contrast favourably with his typically aggressive manner.

On the other hand, I might be reluctant to share a spot with Ron Reagan.

I was once asked to speak in a televised church service in Key Biscayne, Florida. 'Sure,' I said, until I found out that the two speakers before me were to be Billy Graham and the President of the United States. There was no way I was going to follow those two.

You could be expected to answer questions at the end of a hostile film with only a couple of minutes to speak. If you are not briefed properly, it will be virtually impossible to counter such a negative message.

How much influence you have over your television appearance depends on your personal standing and how badly the television company wants you. But there are always a couple of important points. If you are going to be asked to reply to, or discuss, points raised in a piece of film, *make sure* you see it beforehand. Similarly, ask to see any inserts that are going to be put into the programme. You can also expect to be told the general area of questioning, but not the specific questions you will be asked.

You can certainly seek an assurance that any 'noddy' shots (clips of you nodding taken for editing purposes) will not be shown apparently as an answer to a question, when you would, in reality, have answered 'no'. It's happened! In any event, take a small cassette recorder with you and record all that you say and do on a pre-edited interview.

With live broadcasts these problems don't arise because the programme can't be edited. But live broadcasting brings its own dangers - you can be tempted to show off or be too rash. There's no second chance in live television.

You are in control

On television - be deliberate. Almost anything is well received by the viewers as long as they feel that you intended to do or say it.

Compare it to ice-skating. If you go to an ice spectacular and watch Torville and Dean, you expect a certain kind of performance. Even the weeniest wobble from one of them makes you catch your breath because you know it was not supposed to happen. But when the clowns come on, in *Holiday on Ice*, they trip and almost fall hundreds of times, but you are laughing and clapping because you know the trips and the staggers are deliberate and that is exactly what they intended.

So on television you need to be perceived as being in control of yourself - and the situation. If you need to cough, blow your nose or scratch your head, do it, but do it purposefully. Don't dab your nose surreptitiously twenty times or continue speaking through a frog in your throat. Turn a little away from the microphone (to avoid blasting the eardrums of the sound engineer), cough or blow your nose, say 'Excuse me' and carry right on.

If you need to consult some notes or a document to make a point, do it openly, don't glance down at them out of the corner of your eye, it looks dreadfully shifty. You can even think - as long as you *look* as if you're thinking (thought is not banned on TV), not just stuck for words.

I mentioned earlier that television is visual. It's only when you *see* something for the first time that you realise the impact it makes. When television comes to the House of Commons, for example, the behaviour of Members will change. Not necessarily dramatically or even immediately, but it will change. A constituent will ask his Member why he wasn't in the House for an important debate, or why he had his feet up, or why he was yelling when that 'nice Mr so-and-so' was speaking. Whatever restrictions are put on broadcasting the House, these things *will* emerge.

Members and Ministers will need to be more concise, more intelligible in their speeches, to headline and explain the topics for millions of viewers rather than the few hundred other Members of Parliament. If they want to be sure that the right sections of their speeches, with the right emphasis, are seen on their regional television, they will have to prepare their participation with 'sound bites' - sharp concise sections which give a clear picture and fit neatly into programmes.

What should happen in time is that a degree of decorum will take a little of the 'edge' off Commons debates and we should all find out a little more about what our representatives do there. It will bring Members closer to the people they represent. What will *not* happen, in the longer term after the initial 'premiere performances', is that the House of Commons becomes a 'showy' TV studio. People at home will be able to see through it!

Pointing to the message

In a television interview you can say 'Let me think about that for a moment' and pause. You can comfortably take three seconds, sometimes even longer if you're, say, looking at the interviewer with a twinkle in your eye - or a similarly appropriate gesture! But once a viewer *thinks* you're stuck for words, he becomes distracted from your content and that's bad presentation.

The whole art of presentation is to make it easy for the speaker to present the message and easy for the listener to receive it.

The principle of no distraction from your message applies whether you're on TV yourself or arranging an event that will get television coverage. A lot of my time is spent planning major conferences and rallies which will be subject to the scrutiny of the camera. For main speeches I focus all the attention on the speaker so that his or her message will have the maximum visual impact. I brief other members of the platform party (usually far too many) not to do anything that will catch the eye of the viewer - especially pick their noses! If they want to adjust their ties, fan themselves with the programme or get up and go to the loo, they can get it all over with before-hand.

The principle applies to objects as well as people. There was almost a noticeable gaff at the 1988 Institute of Directors

Convention when Marmaduke Hussey addressed them in the Albert Hall. Stuck up behind the speaker's position was a large digital clock which was directly in shot of most floor cameras. The Chairman of the BBC would have appeared on the News that night, with the viewers saying 'Oh, look at the clock, it's 3.30, that must have been this afternoon' and so on. By the time they'd got that out of their systems the ninety-second clip would have been over. But . . . we raised the clock higher and changed the camera angles just in time.

The goal is to get people to concentrate on what *we want them to*. I'm sure Duke Hussey did not want them to concentrate on the clock at the back of his head.

Lights and things

It helps if you know something about the way television works, as it will affect your behaviour; but then relax and forget it. Lighting affects what you wear. Checks, spots, stripes, strong contrasting lines give the camera a nervous breakdown - or 'strobe' as the technical term has it.

Avoid black and white in any quantity. Pastels are good; but nothing too bright. If you have a dazzling white shirt you want to wear, put it in the wash with a tea bag: it will go a kinder shade of off-white.

Take care with your appearance. Look tidy without looking dandy. Simple lines are better than fussy ones (frilly blouses or silk handkerchiefs in top pockets). Dress as casually as you can, while feeling genuinely comfortable in that particular situation.

Untidiness distracts and suggests you're not bothered. Simple jewellery is fine but not big bright brooches which catch and reflect the light. Hair should be washed and neat, women's make-up normal. Pull jackets down at the back and leave them undone. Avoid waistcoats, they look pompous and give you a bulging wrinkled stomach when you are seated. The studio make-up people will check you out.

Most interview shots are from mid-chest to top of head, but

you will want to take care with your lower half as you may be seen full length at some point. Knee-length skirts for women, and men should make sure that the hairy pink gap between bottom of trouser and top of sock is very small. And don't leave your socks rumpled down at the top of your shoe - pull them up.

Studio lights are cooler nowadays so you should not find yourself hot and sweaty, but it's still a good idea to keep clothing relatively lightweight. Arrive early, have time to relax, gather the thoughts and take time for your eyes to become accustomed to the lights (otherwise you could find yourself sneezing or squinting). At conferences where I know speakers will be facing bright lights out on stage, I put the same strength lights in the backstage room to get them used to the glare.

Ignore the microphone once its level has been checked, but don't move your chair or swivel around in it. Sound and lighting will have been set up for that position and it looks 'nervous'.

I say 'ignore' the microphone but do keep your voice funnelling in its direction. Most mikes have a 'V' pick up and if you want to talk to a panel member to your right or left, move your body in the opposite direction and talk *across* the 'V' of the mike rather than away from it.

If you're going to sneeze or hiccup, however, turn away from the mike!

Here's looking at you

Now the camera! Forget about it unless you deliberately choose to acknowledge its presence. The rule in television is the same as in ordinary conversation - *look at the person you're talking to.* If you're being interviewed, look at your interviewer. In that situation, the audience and viewers are in a fly-on-the-wall position.

A good guide for eye contact is that you should make it about fifty per cent of the time. Too little and it looks as if you're trying to avoid meeting someone's eyes; too much and

NATURALLY SPEAKING

The ITN cameras covered 'live' my rescue from the rubble just below the fifth floor of the Grand Hotel in Brighton in 1984. I was only wearing a tee-shirt, matted to my body like an additional skin after being buried in rubble for two and a half hours.

I was instantly covered with a blanket but I had no idea that my rescue and the interviews were being seen worldwide until an old friend in California, Diane Ruby, phoned to say that she'd seen the rescue on American television. Throughout the day other friends called from all over the world - Australia and New Zealand, the Far East, even that wonderful man, the late Bishop Festo Kivengere, who had heard my interview in Africa.

The lesson was rammed home to me. When I spoke about my rescue and my Christian faith from that stretcher in Brighton, I was speaking naturally, from the heart. Because my eyes had been closed for nearly three hours under the muck and rubble, the moment that one television light was put in my face I couldn't see a thing, and I had no idea that there were a dozen or more international television crews filming the interview.

I didn't put it on. I didn't do anything 'special'. I just told the story as I knew it.

Watching those interviews later, re-emphasised the basis of all my teaching in television training - don't perform, just tell it as it is!

you end up staring like a madman. And only look into one of your interviewer's eyes at a time. Trying to look into both at once makes you go cross-eyed.

The rule of looking at who you're talking to applies in most situations. If you're in front of a studio audience (BBC's *Question Time*, for instance), you would look at them as well as the Panel.

You may find yourself on what is known as a down-the-line interview: you are in one studio and your interviewer is in another. He faces you on screen, you face him via the camera, so in this situation you look directly into the camera. The same applies to programmes which need you to address the camera directly like Channel 4's *Comment*, political broadcasts or community access television.

There may be occasions when you want to use the camera openly as a tool of communication. I saw Neil Kinnock interviewed once - he was referring to something someone had said about him. He turned round, asked 'Where's the camera?', looked directly into it and said: 'Now, if you're watching, you'll know that that simply isn't true.' He was obeying the first presentational principle of doing something deliberately and confidently.

Sometimes when I'm talking on television about techniques, I demonstrate this. I turn to the camera and say, 'I must tell you this at home too . . .'

Don't be over-awed at the thought of the 'millions out there'. Television is an intimate personal medium. You are with one or two people in a studio; you're being watched by small groups of individuals in their homes.

Co-ordinating the body

Body language plays a big part in television communication. It says much more than your words by themselves. The words and content are your concrete foundation, but they are thick and boring without the house built on them.

Sit well back in your chair, reasonably upright and make sure your head is not tilted backwards. (It makes you appear to be looking down your nose at everyone.) Lean slightly forward, not enough to appear aggressive. Don't cross your arms - it's a defensive sign and, for some reason, intertwining your fingers distorts them on camera.

Put one hand on top of the other if you're resting them in your lap, and don't fiddle with your button or your ring. If you wear glasses and you really do want to remove them, do it - but I advise against using them as a prop. Either you look as if you're trying to be too clever or else they become an unnecessary distraction.

'Distraction' is the key negative word in any communication. *Steer clear* of anything that distracts your audience from concentrating on your message. *Go ahead* with anything that complements it.

The key to body language is again naturalness, perhaps a slightly exaggerated naturalness. So, if you normally use your hands, use them on television but a fraction more deliberately. If you know it's going to be a tight shot with your head and shoulders, modify gestures a bit, to be in the picture.

Never let a director talk you into being something you are not - for example, by telling you not to move your hands. It may be easier for him not to have to pull a camera back, but that's his problem.

The meat: on-the-air

All these things are important if you appear on television, but neither I nor anyone else can make technique work for you if you have nothing to say. You have to have a message, substance, to communicate. Presentation cannot succeed without content. Your attitude, confidence and tone make ninety per cent of the *impact*, but they *will not carry you on their own*. Your content must be solid.

That means knowing your subject. If you don't you'll be seen for the fool that you are. When you speak be sure your brain has caught up with your mouth. Otherwise you'll either be floundering around for words or have to start waffling and blustering. Either way television will show you up.

The two main set-piece interview styles are *information* or *interrogation*. Obviously the information approach is more relaxed and the questions are more prompts than specifics. But in both cases you must know what you want to say, rehearse how you're going to summarise it and anticipate ways of bringing it legitimately into the conversation.

A summary, a headline, at the *beginning* of every answer in a television interview is essential. With public speaking, radio and television, tell the audience where you are going and only then tell them the route. Avoid one-word answers - unless there is nothing to say except 'yes' or 'no'.

Showing knowledge is not a matter of volume or quantity.

You are not going to get the television equivalent of a 2,000 word article. In an average appearance the maximum you can hope to get is two minutes, time for only one or two points. So, before you go on, distil what you want to communicate and *think* before you speak.

Politicians and public figures often make the mistake of thinking that the viewer is hanging on every word floating from their lips. No way! On television you are selling the sizzle and the quality; you are not asking the viewers to chew through the steak in two minutes. So don't say too much. Cut it down to clear simple language - speak in headlines.

If the interviewer quotes incorrect facts or makes wrong assumptions, correct him - but as you would a colleague, not as an antagonist. Listen to the *full* question and absorb it before you start to answer. By the way, you are not obliged to answer completely hypothetical questions unless it is an advantage to do so. Include them in your rehearsal though, so that you can practise dealing with them.

Most interviewers are reasonably professional and try at least to appear objective. Sadly, though, more and more are allowing editorial or personal bias to get into the questions and staging. Their 'good guys' are seen in a visually interesting location - on the ice saving whales or cleaning ocean pollution from suffering birds. The 'bad guys' are then interviewed in a cold, powerful rich environment, a boardroom or hotel. Thus an impression is given of uncaring blame for the problem - guilty before a question is asked. Then the interview begins: 'Mr so-and-so, how can you *defend* the appalling results from your company's policy of pouring oil waste into the breeding waters of these poor creatures?'

Now if it's true - tough! Don't ask me to sort out your content for you. But if it isn't, get the facts, rehearse your presentation, including *showing* your attitude, and be in a 'sympathetic' location to give your interview.

Don't get flustered and there really is no need to be on the defensive; relax, tell the truth and don't try to 'outsmart' the interviewer.

GOOD IMPRESSION

Early in 1989 I watched the US Secretary of Commerce, Robert Mosbachev, on a live TV interview in Washington DC - down the line from New York.

He was expecting to be questioned only on Japanese-US trade figures, but the first question was: 'Do you think that President Bush's clean, ethical image has been damaged by the investigations into drink and womanising allegations about the nominee for Secretary for Defense?'

With an almost-smile, Mr Mosbachev commented thoughtfully and pleasantly, was quietly reassuring to the viewer and chatted naturally straight into the camera. It was an effective piece of gentle advocacy for the President.

But the interesting thing to me was that his obvious sincerity worked - in spite of a very stiff body position, a striped suit and a black and white checked tie!

'I want to make this absolutely clear'

Television is a multi-faceted channel of communication which is watched in all kinds of circumstances.

People will be eating their supper as they watch, or flipping through a magazine with the children playing and making a noise. You have to catch their attention above all the distractions. Even when they do look at the screen, they are as likely to be musing on the colour of your tie or criticising your hairstyle as pondering the flowery flannel you are spouting. That will come last of all. You have to earn the viewers' attention. They don't owe you anything.

Then there's waffle! As a species, politicians seem particularly vulnerable to this disease, wheeling in tired old clichés like 'the fact of the matter is', 'in real terms', 'at the end of the day', 'at this moment in time' and 'you have to understand that . . .' Such phrases are rubbish - waffle used by people who either haven't done their homework or haven't rehearsed and prepared enough.

Please do not be afraid to rehearse - in front of the mirror, in front of your family or friends if they will give you honest criticism, in front of a video camera if possible.

Speak in your normal voice, talking to the other person, not the microphone. Vary your delivery by changing pace, tone and volume. Avoid a continuous, boring monotone. Train yourself to speak without stuttering and hesitation, but avoid a delivery that is too smooth. My friend David Wickes, script-writer and film producer, comments: 'To err is human, to er . . . er . . . is boring'. Talk naturally, be human, relax and concentrate. Use anecdotes and humour wherever possible; be able to laugh at yourself and give the viewer something memorable if you can.

Be courteous and informal but without being over-familiar. Address your interviewer or co-interviewee in whatever form you would if talking off camera, but don't contrive to keep dragging their names in artificially.

Conversations should be like a game of ping-pong, back and forth, so don't drone on or hog the air time. If someone else *is* doing that and you need to interrupt, wait until he takes a breath and then cut in with a real comment, short and to the point, and don't stop talking until you have made it.

Keep off jargon if you can but when it's unavoidable, give a quick definition. Say the term and then add 'Which as you may know refers to . . .' or 'By which I mean . . .' You will have done most viewers (and probably the interviewer) a favour. They will have learned something and you will have avoided alienating them by sounding pompous.

In rehearsal, be sure someone throws the nastier questions at you so that you can think through your answer.

There is never any need to appear defensive: if you know what you want to say and how you want to say it, you can make the most thorny subject work for you.

Hearts first

Above all, remember that you want to win the person, not just the argument. Aim at the emotions first and follow up with the facts.

You cannot answer emotional questions with statistics alone. You wouldn't try to convince a close friend or your spouse simply by bombarding them with figures. It is possible to out-argue someone because you know you're right and you have all the material at your fingertips, but still lose the person.

The idea is not to browbeat or make people feel uneasy, guilty or out-thought. When we use the expression 'winning their hearts and minds' - hearts come first!

Tell a story and create a picture in the viewer's mind that will stay long after you are off the screen.

That's cool

An interviewer will try to keep the initiative over you but although they ask questions with authority (that's their job), they know much less about the subject than you do (that's why you're being interviewed). With some interviewers, the less they know about something, the more forcefully they tend to probe.

Only get angry deliberately - 'This makes me very angry and I'll tell you why'; if you really lose your temper, you have lost control. If you reach a point where you think the interviewer or an opponent is being unreasonable say something like, 'Now, I've done my very best to answer this point and there's really nothing else I can add.'

Keep your cool and avoid sounding frustrated or, worse, petulant. The viewer will side with the interviewer first in a confrontation because he feels he 'knows' him. So if you nag or harangue or hector the interviewer, you'll lose the viewer's sympathy.

Respond thoughtfully to another point of view in arguing your case and anticipate when a discussion is drawing to a close so that you can finish on a positive note. In some circumstances, it will make more impact if you let opponents have the last word - for example, if they're going to behave in an aggressive or domineering fashion that will reflect badly on them!

Because television is so personal, aggressiveness, irritation, bad humour and arrogance rebound on the speaker. Who wants a nasty character in their home? Good television performance comes from applying the correct principles and practice, not from shallow techniques and tricks.

Whoops

Most of the things I've discussed so far are for when you appear on television or radio voluntarily.

There is another situation. It's what is known in the business as 'doorstepping' - because camera crews and reporters wait on the 'doorstep' for someone, or accost them walking along the street. At your home or place of work, or as you go into a meeting or a courtroom, you suddenly find cameras rolling and a microphone thrust up your nose. You don't want to say anything; indeed, in some circumstances you *must* not say anything, but you have to make some response.

To start with, never use the expression 'no comment': it looks sullen and defensive and sounds foolish.

There are all kinds of ways of saying nothing in a polite and courteous fashion; politicians do it all the time. Exchange pleasantries and explain that you may be in a position to talk later but 'I know you'll understand that I can't say anything at all at the moment'. Anything as long as you avoid that dreadful cliché 'no comment'. The soft answer turneth away wrath (Proverbs 15 Verse 1).

Business television

To add to the growing number of broadcast television opportunities, the big increase in owners of video cassette recorders and new awareness of the impact of a moving picture in communications, has brought a huge new market - corporate or business videos.

It was really the pop world that first realised that by adding vision to sound and written words, the product leaps to life. A business or sales message that may require thousands of printed words or dozens of meetings to get across, can hit home to everybody in a ten-minute video. Companies are now using business video for a whole number of purposes: a 'teaser' for a new product launch; an introduction to a company and its people for potential clients; in-house training programmes or even as back-up graphs and comment for reports to investors.

There is one common denominator for business and broadcast television: it must be entertaining and professional to make

---

TELEVISION SUMMARY

Prepare

1 Before you accept an invitation to go on television find out:
   a) What is the *subject*, do you *know* the subject, why have they invited *you*?
   b) What is the programme, who is the interviewer, who else is taking part, what is the format, is it live or recorded, will it be edited?
   c) Where, when and for how long are you needed? How long will your final contribution be?
   d) Who are the viewers (national, regional, specialist)?
2 When you have accepted the invitation, study the subject and pick out one or two points that you want to get across. Then work out ways of bringing them into your conversation with the interviewer. Prepare some headlines. Rehearse potentially tough questions.
3 Take trouble with your appearance. Wash your hair. Shave (if necessary). Clean your teeth. Choose clothing with simple lines, avoid 'fussiness' - handkerchief in top pocket, frilly dresses, etc. Pull your jacket down at the back and leave it undone. Keep jewellery simple. Look tidy not dandy. Avoid sharply contrasting colours, stripes, checks or black and white. Pick blues, greys or pastel colours without sharp patterns.

In the studio

1 Assume that *everything* you say and do can be seen and heard by the public.
2 Sit well back in the chair, reasonably upright, and make sure that your head is not tilted backwards.
3 Look at the studio lights for a few minutes before the interview so that you're not squinting when it begins.

an impact on the selected audience. The huge developing market in corporate videos has to meet the same standards of technical and programme levels as the broadcast companies.

This means not only more opportunities for production companies, writers and directors, but an ever increasing need for company executives to learn how to present themselves effectively. The impact of the medium is increasing in scope

---

4 Look at the person to whom you are talking or listening. If that person is 'down the line', *only then* do you talk to the camera.

'On air'
1 Think - take time for it.
2 It's your *attitude* that makes the big impression - rarely your words!
3 *Be personal* - courteous but always informal. You are talking to the interviewer and one or two people in a living room, not 'millions of people out there'.
4 Talk naturally, *don't* use jargon. Headline. Be human. Use illustrations and anecdotes. Aim at the heart first and then drop in factual support. Avoid long words, long sentences and long lists.
5 There is *never* an occasion when you will *have to* appear defensive. Use the interviewer. Don't allow him to make you appear to be 'the enemy'.
6 Relax - but concentrate. Keep it simple.

Before and after
1 If there are any inserts, interviews or films on which you will have to comment, see them *before* you go on-air.
2 Coffee, tea or soft drinks *before* broadcasting. Never alcohol! Broadcasting is like driving - a drop of alcohol and you're more dangerous than useful. You will, however, be able to come back to the Green Room (hospitality) *after* the programme.
3 Remember - when you're inside a TV building, cameras and microphones could be running, even after the interview when you think you are 'off-the-air'.

---

and importance. The best people being head-hunted will judge a company first by what they see in its corporate video. Chairmen who cannot meet hundreds of employees will keep their loyalty or lose it through a corporate video.

In times of corporate crisis, a company chief can and will have to reach all of his employees in dozens of national or international locations *simultaneously* in a live link.

Looking towards the European single market economy at the beginning of 1993, the decision-makers in British business and industry are recognising both the impact and the cost effectiveness of video - and the fact that it can give the same message at the same time to employees and associates in different countries, and in different languages.

The message is - prepare now! At the end of the 1980s it is not yet a 'have to' situation. By 1995 it will be!

'Allo 'Allo

There's a lot of similarity in performance between television and radio, but clearly your voice, tone, pace etc, has to do *all* the work on the radio. There's the same need to prepare and practise, speak confidently and deliberately, to be aware of the technology and, at the same time, to ignore it.

In radio, too, you need to know your programme's format (discussion, phone-in, interview, panel) *and* something about your listeners.

But you don't have vision! Your appearance can neither help nor hinder; your voice presentation and solid message is it! Your voice has to be interesting. Use variations of tone and pace and when you want to emphasise a point, speak slowly and slightly more softly. You are talking to another person, usually as he or she is doing something else like driving or housework: you are *not* addressing a mass of people.

Radio is greatly underrated as a means of communication. People get carried away by the 'glamour' of television and forget that you can reach millions on radio. It is a great forum for sowing and watering ideas, giving the written press some fodder for expansion and setting the agenda - taking the initiative on the subject you want to present.

The same way that British Midland Airway's Michael Bishop did an excellent job on television after the M1 crash in early 1989, the Boeing representative on Radio 4's *Today* with John Humphreys was appalling. He was in Seattle and his cold, defensive suspicious attitude came over my car radio like a storm. I don't remember any of his actual words but what I 'heard' was - 'Don't start questioning Boeing. We're the biggest plane makers in the world and you British ought to remember that because you rely on us for most of your flying.' No concern was communicated in his voice for the dead or injured. No urgency came through as regards helping search for the cause of the crash. Just arrogance. Two days later faulty wiring was discovered in some other Boeings!

As with television, local radio is going to keep on multiplying in the nineties. These stations are hungry for news and, perhaps above all, for the personal interview. Most national figures are interviewed only by the networks, and local radio stations need to maximise their use of local people.

Because radio is 'voice only' it is easy to slacken on preparation. Don't. However there are some benefits with radio. It is cheaper and easier for them to come and interview you, either live or on tape, than it is with television and that can help in a busy schedule.

You can also be more casually dressed. I do a lot of telephone interviews from Europe with the Moody Network from Chicago - some one hundred radio stations across America. Because of the time difference - we are six hours ahead of Chicago - I am usually sitting up in bed on the phone for my interviews. On one occasion I was in bed having a live conversation with people in Washington, Chicago and Los Angeles - all in studios. At the 1988 National Religious Broadcasters Convention in Washington DC, I did a live interview on the Moody network with Jim Warren and Melinda Schmidt. I started - 'You know, this is the first time I've done an interview with you when I'm wearing clothes.' I did explain to the listeners!

Use the same conversational technique in a phone-in radio discussion as you would in person. Headline - keep your points few and simple. On radio, however, you will need to explain some things a little more. I had to explain to listeners that I was usually in bed in London when I spoke to them but that this time I was 'live' - and dressed - in Washington.

Because you cannot be seen by the viewers there can be far more activity in a radio studio than around the cameras, albeit quiet activity. I was a guest on a Los Angeles radio show with the Mayor of LA. We were discussing in some detail the different campaigning techniques in Europe and America. A young lady silently shoved a handwritten note in front of me. My concentration went totally as I looked down expecting an important instruction. It read 'Cream and sugar in your coffee?'

Enunciation - speaking clearly - is more important on radio. On the screen viewers can see your expression and your lip movement.

In writing 'Enunciation - speaking clearly - is etc' in the previous paragraph, I have just used a useful radio technique. It was not *assuming* that you did not know what enunciation meant. It was partly to reinforce the word but mostly just *in case* you didn't know it.

To avoid overtly patronising explanations you can slip in such a reinforcer which also explains, and the thousands who don't know are suddenly (and discreetly) enlightened. They are grateful not only because they have learned but also because they have not had to admit that they didn't understand. It's useful on television too.

Finally, on-mike, you need just that much more expression and enthusiasm in your voice. Because there is less time to think on radio than television, it is even more important, to *know* the points you want to get across - and *how* you will present them.

Listen to the radio, get familiar with the format, before you go on.

'That wasn't so bad - was it?'

OK, so a lot of what I have talked about is easier preached than performed. Television and radio sometimes terrify people to the point of panic, but there is no reason at all why you should not approach them with confidence.

RADIO SUMMARY

Listeners are eavesdropping on your talking to the interviewer or phone-in caller.

Prepare

a) Have a clear personal objective for your radio appearance.

b) Be aware of whether your programme is live or recorded and whether it is to be edited.

c) Prepare your subject, headlines and key points as you would for television.

d) Know the key areas of questions or discussion.

e) Plan for the type of programme - interview, phone-in, discussion.

f) Be aware of your target audience - eg national or regional, housewives or young people.

On air

a) You are speaking to a person not a meeting, so talk to the people not a microphone - but don't sway away from the mike.

b) Ping pong conversation – don't drone on – speak colloquially; headline.

c) If you must interrupt, wait for the speaker to breathe and then come in firmly with a real comment - short and to the point.

d) To emphasise a point, speak more slowly and slightly more softly.

e) Vary your tone, your voice level and speed. The listener has nothing else to help receive your communication.

Confidence comes from preparation, practice and professional advice. I'm often asked if I think 'stage fright' is a good thing or not. Isn't it better to have some 'butterflies' before a public performance?

You have to separate stage fright from adrenalin. Adrenalin gears you up to peak performance and people perform best when it's flowing. But you don't want the kind of stage fright that leaves you a stuttering, waffling wreck. Much of it is an individual response, some people are more nervous than others; you are not obliged to fit into any particular pattern.

However, *never* take alcohol to 'calm your nerves'. That's not just the teetotal preacher talking, even the smallest amount is enough to slur your speech, dull your mind even more, and make you sweat under lights! You can take advantage of the hospitality suite afterwards if you wish. Drink tea, coffee or a soft drink but not *iced* water, which constricts the throat.

Finally, a last cautionary note, for both television and radio. Always assume while you're in the studio and its surrounding areas that anything you say or do can be seen or heard by the public.

There was a wonderful moment with Derek Hatton, the militant city councillor in Liverpool, when he'd finished a local radio interview. After he left the room he started to make remarks like, 'Well, I'm glad so-and-so never came up' and 'What a relief they never asked about X'. Unfortunately for him, he was still wearing his radio mike - and it was still switched on! Sadly, the professionals *were* professional and the public never got to hear the comments.

President Reagan was not so fortunate. In a perfectly legitimate mike-test he joked that 'Bombing of Russia will begin tomorrow'. In a disgraceful breach of professional etiquette, they broadcast his comments.

Mike-tests are there for fun, but what they say about truth and jests is right. I often test microphones at conferences by observing that my words are likely to be the most interesting heard at the conference - or that 'In a remarkable precedent, three people woke up during yesterday's session!' Many a true word spoken, etc!

Good professionals don't let you down - and if they do, it rebounds on them more than you. So enjoy your sound checks!

On the panel

A few pointers for the radio or television panel discussion.

A good host will make sure that everyone gets a fair say and you *ought* not to have to fight too much.

Keep notes as you go. Write down the names of questioners in the audience so that you can refer to them personally. Note the opposing points to yours so that you can summarise them when it's your turn to comment.

If it becomes necessary to chime in, don't stop until you have said what you want to! Prepare a clear sharp point, comment or question. Wait for a 'breath' by whoever you have to interrupt and come in firmly and clearly and sounding (and looking) slightly reluctant to interrupt - but not apologetic.

Make the point and stop! Your mike will be on. A camera will switch to you - if it is television - and you will not lose the sympathy of the audience if you are brief and courteous.

And finally, whatever the programme format and your contribution to it, ask yourself . . . were you interesting? Radio and television must be entertaining. If you are dull or boring - *nothing* can save you!

Part Two
SPECIAL EVENTS

4
THE GRAND DESIGN

Nothing great was ever achieved without enthusiasm.

Ralph Waldo Emerson

Those old Andy Hardy movies always seemed to have a scene where a bunch of American teenagers would be sitting around in an old barn or something wondering where to stage their amateur dramatics. Suddenly one would leap onto a bale of hay and exclaim, 'I know, kids, why don't we do the show right here . . .?' There would be a couple of quick scenes of frenzied activity and then they would cut to a grand finale of Mickey Rooney & Co singing and dancing their way across a barn miraculously transformed into a splendid stage.

This is the kind of dreamy Hollywood fantasy I like to float in when I'm lying flat on my back under some dirty platform desperately trying to tack a loose wire or stubborn piece of baize into position - or standing in a wet field trying to work out exactly how the VIPs will swim through the mud from the helicopter to the marquee.

No event just 'happens'; it's got to be created. Whether it is a school fête or a huge rally, a successful event is the result of clear objectives, imagination, planning, an overall view and attention to countless details.

This part of the book will give you an expert - and simple - guide to planning and staging such events. It's based on my experience of presenting thousands of them in close to a hundred countries around the world, under a wide variety of conditions.

I shall be talking mainly about conferences, because they are the most common. There are more than 200,000 a year in the United Kingdom alone. You can go into any reasonable size hotel some days and find two or three events on simultaneously. It is increasingly likely that anyone who takes an active role in *any* organisation will at some point find themselves involved in setting up a 'special event'.

Most of the principles and practicalities we shall be discussing for conferences apply to other events too, but where there are special considerations and differences for, say, rallies or exhibitions, I will mention them.

The key elements are: imagination, planning, foresight, thoroughness and a never-ending willingness to go that 'extra mile' in dealing with people and details. These are as essential when you're planning a company training seminar with twenty-five people as they are when you're organising an 8,000 delegate, fifty-nation, ten-day congress.

Setting the objectives

First of all you must have clear goals, a picture in your mind of how you see the end result and a plan to monitor your progress and results. It's no good going to work on the details unless you have this 'vision'. It would be like taking London's M25 or Washington's beltway, in the hope of getting somewhere; all you would do is go round and round in circles.

You have to know where you're going if you are to plan the best way of getting there!

Before you start, ask yourself: what are our objectives, what message are we trying to get across, which people do we want to reach, what emotions should they feel, what responses are we looking for, what do we want them to take from this event - in person or through the media and press?

A conference may, for instance, be held to *communicate* policy as the Conservative Party's is, or to *decide* policy as in Labour's case. You may wish to inform a specialist group of people, or give them a reward or an incentive.

An exhibition may be aimed at creating new marketing ideas or providing an arena for marketing. A rally may be aimed at exciting, motivating or converting people, and so on. Only when you know *what* you want to achieve can you plan *how* you are going to achieve it. The goal dictates the form.

The goal dictates the form.

It was frustrating at the Brighton Conservative Party Conference in 1988 to find 'entrepreneurs' selling Union Jacks on the afternoon of Mrs Thatcher's address. It was the wrong occasion: the amateur just 'likes flags and razzamatazz' but the professional creates the atmosphere to suit the occasion. This was a mid-term party conference, not a general election rally!

In America they ask: 'What do we want to achieve?' and then: 'How do we achieve it?'

In England we say: 'What shall we do?' and then: 'I wonder if it will achieve anything?'

No wonder we win so few gold medals or cups.

In America the political conventions are designed to enthuse the participants and television viewers to go out and campaign for their candidates for the Presidency and Vice-Presidency. Because that is the aim, razzamatazz, music, flags, balloons, streamers and placards are appropriate means to help achieve it.

I remember during the Republican National Convention in Dallas in 1984 walking through the floor as the renomination of President Reagan was being acclaimed. Thousands of flags were waving, helium balloons were going up and air balloons were coming down, two separate bands at both ends of the huge auditorium were playing different songs and everyone was cheering and screaming their heads off. I was walking quietly by one group of people when a delightful black girl saw me passing and, in the nicest way possible, flung her arms around my neck and said, 'Isn't America wonderful?' The magic had certainly worked for her.

In 1985 there was a double objective for a rally I did with Ernie Guy for the American Bar Association in the Royal Albert Hall. Although it was a major political speech by the Prime Minister, it was quite appropriate to have a military band and flags and a bit of excitement. The Americans expected it and so it *prepared* them to sit down quietly and listen to the speech.

On the other hand, most of the political and commercial conferences that I do are either for presentation on television of important policies or for discussion and debate on serious issues. In such cases too many frills and too much frivolity would be all wrong. The professional plans the presentation to suit the message and achieve the objective - not to 'put on a good show'.

Paying for it

Once you have a clear idea of what you have to do, the next thing is to work out how you pay for it.

There's something of the chicken and egg situation in this. It's hard to decide what you can do if you don't know how much money you can get, and it's hard to decide what something will cost if you haven't a clear idea of what you want to do.

Sort this out at your first planning meeting and much will depend on the particular circumstances of your organisation. It may have unlimited funds or it may have very tight ones; most fall somewhere in between so you have to think creatively about raising the additional finance to do the job properly.

There are several things to remember about finance. One is that the bigger the event (up to about 3,000 people) the more it costs *proportionally*. It is not simply a question of multiplying numbers. For instance, you may find that a conference for seventy people in a smallish London hotel will work out at £30 a head per day. But if you're doing something for 7,000, the costs will be more per person per day. That's because large events involve extra considerations you never dreamed of when doing a small conference.

If you're hiring Earls Court, for example, most people in the audience probably would not even be able to see the speakers, let alone hear them. So you're talking about setting up giant screens and elaborate video and sound systems.

Another important point is that the less time you have in which to do something, the more it costs because you start to run into things like overtime and special delivery payments, rush jobs and so on.

In 1979 we held the United Kingdom's first showbiz-style election rally for Mrs Thatcher, and it was a great success. A few days later Lord Thorneycroft, the Party Chairman, and Alastair (now Lord) McAlpine came to me and asked if we could stage another for the European Elections - three weeks later. We had spent nine months working on the first one!

When I had got my breath back, I said, 'Yes, we can, but it will cost three times as much and the Party will have to be responsible for getting people to come to it.' (The most difficult part of any conference is getting the right number of the right people to attend.) We set to work and produced the rally and it was terrific. It showed you can achieve something at short notice, provided you're prepared to drop everything *and* cover the cost. Petula Clark sang, and political agents wept - with emotion!

Such occasions, however, have to be very special. No-one can operate like that consistently, nor should it be necessary. For any event involving more than two hundred people, a year's planning is just about enough; for any event involving fewer people six months is the absolute minimum.

Work out your initial budget for every possible item of expenditure *and then pad it*. Be as precise and as far-seeing as possible. Many people spend money chronologically rather than strategically, with the result that they run out before they've done everything. A little foresight might have shown them that spending less on early hospitality and a bit more on the venue would have saved them time, money and trouble overall.

Similarly, it's no good discovering that you are going to need an autocue and a slide projector when there's no money left to buy or hire them, or that your guest speaker will only fly first class when you've allocated £200 in your budget for his travel costs because someone vaguely remembered that £200 was the 'Apex fare'.

When you're inviting speakers, discover what their real needs are going to be. It's not unknown for an American to want to show a dozen video tapes, each of which may cost £50 to transfer to the British system.

Plan your expenditure for each stage. For instance, site recces. I make it a rule to go at least three times. Allow for such visits and the travel and accommodation costs they entail. If you're borrowing money for the event, be it £200 or £20,000, include the interest payments as part of your expenditure budget.

Insure against everything from salmonella poisoning to a speaker's non-appearance, and keep finances for a particular event separate from the company or organisation's general finances.

Once you've drawn up this highly detailed (and incredibly efficient) list, pad it. Pad every section by ten per cent at least. The smaller the overall budget, the more you pad to give yourself room for manoeuvre. I'd recommend padding a budget of under £1,000 by at least fifty per cent.

And after you've done all the item padding, allow *another* fifteen per cent for contingencies. The odds are that you will have to dip into it, but if you don't, and you come in under budget, everyone else will be enormously impressed by your professionalism.

Many events will in fact generate an income to offset some of the expense - perhaps a registration fee, a commercial exhibition or sales of souvenirs. The point is to be specific about income and to plan it to meet your *maximum* budget.

It always strikes me as odd that we are incredibly specific in our lives about the small things, ordering a sandwich for instance: we order type of bread, filling, relish, seasonings and extras. But when it comes to big things like religion, politics and money, we all too often just vaguely hope that we'll get by.

Don't 'muddle through' when you're planning an event. Don't say, 'Oh, if we have a wine and cheese party, it'll bring something in', when you need to be sure of raising £300. Nor is it any good hoping you'll raise all the money at the conference itself if three-quarters of the bills have to be paid beforehand. You have to make things happen, not let them get mentioned, discussed and then forgotten.

Who does what

Who actually does what will depend on the nature of your organisation, whether, for instance, it is part of a professional set-up drawing on different departments, resources and personnel within a company, or whether it is purely voluntary - or a mixture of both.

In any conference or special event there are certain essentials. You *must* have a co-ordinator who liaises between the different people, takes the overall view, is good at detail and is ultimately the person with whom 'the buck stops'.

Find a secretary and some key workers, depending on your needs. You should also have a treasurer or accountant to supervise the spending of the money and a finance chairman to raise it. (These two functions ought to be separate. The accountant cannot be worrying about money coming in. He needs to have time and freedom to concentrate on proper spending!)

For bigger events you may also need someone to look after travel and accommodation, the programme, publicity and, most important, a person responsible for getting the right people to enrol, always the most difficult single task.

These are a few suggestions. Your event will have its own needs and the composition of the committee may be suggested accordingly.

Oh good - a committee

Committee? Now there's a word to chill the blood! If Moses had been a committee, the Children of Israel would still be in Egypt. But you need a body that can get together at various stages to liaise and swap ideas but whose members can function in their independent tasks.

I have included here a planning chart for small conferences which has served as a basis for hundreds of other charts I've used over the years. You can adapt it for your own taste but keep the pointers in mind.

Once you've had your initial meeting, drawn up your central strategy and agreed your budget, individuals should be allowed to get on with their jobs with a reasonable amount of flexibility.

CONFERENCE PREPARATION CHART

	7 Months	24–21 Wks	20–17 Wks	16–13 Wks
Executive Secretary	– Confirm committee/s – Confirm site – Assess insurance needs – Print special letterhead + news release paper – Arrange site visit – Draft printing schedule	– Committee meeting – Prepare news release data for labels	– Arrange 2nd site visit	– Committee meetin – Visit key reps PROMOTIO
Arrangements		– Visit site – Confirm contract – Pay deposit – Meet local authorities – Decide on exhibition	– Arrange insurance – Announce exhibition – Appoint exhibition contractor	– Draft detailed arrangements, including venue office, sound, TV crowd flow – Exhibition design
Finance	– Draft budget – Open conference account	– Finalise budget/income – Confirm payment methods – Agree registration fees	– Solicit donations	– Seek some larger donors – Contact potential sponsors
Publicity	– Draft publicity time-table – Compile media list	– General press announcement – Establish local media contacts – Local radio announcements	– Print leaflets – News release (main subjects and speakers) – Contact exhibition customers	– News release (major and new programme participants) – Leaflet to membe – Announce exhibition
Enrolment/ Participants	– Plan total attendance	– Announcement to members plus form – Appoint 'reps' for recruitment	– Solicit for recommended participants – Announce programme highlights to members	– News bulletin wit leaflet + form – Announce group possibilities
Travel/ Accommodation		– Book hotels – Survey external & local travel facilities	– Preliminary travel bookings	– Book local travel facilities
Programme	– Draft outline programme chart	– Select and invite speakers – Confirm main subjects/motions	– Invite any 'special guests'	– Explore follow-up possibilities – Draft spouse programme

12–9 Wks	8–5 Wks	4–2 Wks	1 Wk
Visit key reps TRAVELS	– Committee meeting	– Committee meeting – Prepare key outlet news release envelopes	– On site committee meeting – Overview check of all activities
Re-visit site Plan: seating, parking, signs Note: PA, recording facilities, video, AV Assign rooms Plan venue office	– Prepare final check lists, inc. exhibition – Check insurance – Book telephones and fax – Recruiting letter for stewards	– Appoint stewards – Finalise all exhibition details – Print signs – Confirm venue office details	– Check lists – Briefing meetings – Rehearsals – Open venue office, phones, fax, photocopiers
Confirm venue arrangements costs Plan promotional sales items – pens etc.	– Meeting to compare budget income & expenditure – Confirm sponsorship arrangements	– Reminder letter for unpaid fees – Budget/income assessment – Further approach to donors	– Collection during conference
Local radio/press stories Appoint event photographer	– News release (number enrolled) – Letter prominent local organisations + individuals – Assess programme's TV potential	– News release (final plans) – Press information on facilities at conference – Contact TV	– Local radio/press interviews – Daily releases to key outlets – TV interviews – Press conference
Invite recommended participants 30% enrolled "Bring one other" campaign Push group bookings	– Final reminder bulletin + form – 50% enrolled – Invite observers – Invite donors and sponsors	– 75% enrolled – Announce 'public' meetings	– Registration – Late enrolment
Adjust travel and accommodation bookings	ASSIGN ACCOMMODATIONS		
	– Confirm local travel arrangements	– Meet local travel people	– Rehearsals on local travel arrangements
– Plan excursions & socials – Programme participants' meeting	– Approve final programme – Print programme – Develop follow-up – Confirm spouse programme	– Appoint follow-up personnel – Confirm meeting rooms	– Select 'emergency' motions – Make necessary adjustments

Don't put yourself in a situation where the treasurer has to come back to the committee to argue over every last penny.

To take a simple illustration. If it's been agreed that the treasurer spends £300 on publicity with £100 each for posters, leaflets and newspaper advertisements, he should be allowed the latitude to spend £150 on newspaper ads and £150 on leaflets if the publicity chairman thinks it necessary, and perhaps nothing on posters.

Don't schedule too many meetings. The trouble is, organisers love 'em! One of my bigger irritations is when I have an enormously tight schedule taking me all over the country and I get calls - sometimes on my mobile phone when I'm stuck in the middle of a field somewhere - insisting that it's vitally important I attend a meeting that has just been scheduled for three o'clock that afternoon in London, which could easily have been planned at least two weeks earlier.

When you're drawing up the timetable right at the beginning there is no reason why you cannot fix your planning meeting dates, and stick pretty closely to them. There are rare occasions when emergency meetings are necessary but such crises are nearly always avoidable if people are working well and the schedule has been properly organised.

I had to hold some emergency meetings once, during the preparations for Billy Graham's Euro 70 Crusade at Dortmund in 1970. Billy was suddenly taken quite ill and all our closed circuit television centres around Europe had to be briefed quickly - and in person. I scheduled airport meetings in fourteen of the thirty-six centres and travelled to seven on each of two days. The first day it was Kristiansand, Oslo, Copenhagen, Hamburg, Amsterdam, London and Brussels. Late at night I drove to Germany and the next day met committees in Frankfurt, Paris, Geneva, Zegreb, Graz, Munich and Vienna. Most of the trip was on scheduled flights - all exactly on time!

Of course, you do need to monitor people once they have been given their tasks. You can't just go away and hope everything will fall into place.

I was once involved in setting up ten Crusades simultaneously in Australia and New Zealand for Billy Graham. They were about 3,500 miles apart and I was visiting each one at least once a month for a year. That meant I was travelling a route that stretched from Darwin in northern Australia to Invercargill in southern New Zealand. At one team meeting Billy asked me if all the travelling, and the time and money it took, were really necessary. I told him it was and he said fine.

Nearly two years later he told me that in each of those ten Crusades, people on the committees had said that, although everyone had agreed on certain tasks to be done, they only actually got cracking on them a couple of days before I was due back!

That kind of effort is worthwhile, because it motivates and energises workers. There is no substitute for personal contact in this work.

If you are an event co-ordinator giving your personal direction, passing on *your* commitment and gut-level conviction is vital. If an organiser does not co-ordinate and monitor and know exactly what's going on at each stage, then ultimately he has only himself to blame if something goes wrong.

You can never plan too much, never work out too many details or anticipate too many 'worst cases'. It helps you understand other people's tasks, avoid problems and keep in mind that crucial overview I spoke of earlier.

Your event has a personality!

Perhaps this is the point at which to mention an event's atmosphere, its charisma, its personality, if you like. It's a hard thing to talk about and difficult to define, but it is that essence that makes an event special, different from the rest, even from similar occasions in other years.

Sometimes it happens spontaneously. At other times you have to create it, perhaps by one imaginative stroke, perhaps by hundreds of tiny details: programme decoration, colour scheme, logos, motifs, slogans, guests, music, menus and so on.

At the Conservative Party Conference in Brighton in 1988 we had a little fun on the last day, just before the Prime Minis-

---

FIRST NIGHT

Planning the huge Billy Graham Crusades of the sixties and seventies meant starting from scratch and moving into a city or country six to eighteen months ahead.

The 'first night' was always a little tense and emotional as we saw hundreds come forward at the end of the service to commit their lives to Christ. I would usually be at the foot of the platform stairs as Billy went on at the start. Behind him was the vice-president of the organisation, Walter Smyth.

All of us in the team knew that we were totally dependent on the Lord for any 'success' – but it was still reassuring at each crusade when Walter would murmur to me as he surveyed the huge first night crowds - 'Well, Harvey, that's your job safe till the next one!'

---

ter's speech. The audience was sitting waiting, about forty-five minutes before the start. I asked our organist, Douglas Reeves, to switch to the rhythmic, sing-along songs. People began to clap and wave flags. I turned our closed circuit cameras onto the flag-wavers and they appeared on the huge screens above the stage. As the audience saw themselves on screen they began to 'perform' for the cameras and within minutes the whole audience was cheering, singing and even dancing in the aisles.

In two minutes we had created the excitement, fun and audience involvement that set the atmosphere for the afternoon. When the Prime Minister came to speak we had quietened it down so that they were ready to listen. Object achieved!

If you agree on the details and choose a theme you can then weave them into your planning at every stage.

Working backwards

When you are compiling a flow-chart, work backwards! For example: you want to produce some leaflets about an event that is happening on July 21. You need time for the leaflets to be effective - maybe three weeks. You allow a week to ten days to distribute them, so they have to be ready on June 15.

Allowing for running and folding time, proof correction,

author's corrections, design and scripting, it soon becomes clear that by early-May you must be sitting down to plan the details of those leaflets - no later. It would be useless to start compiling the leaflets at the beginning of July, but that's what often happens.

This is just one example. Apply the same countdown procedure to other elements, and over-estimate how long things will take rather than under-estimate. That way you can only be pleasantly surprised - occasionally.

A flow chart, compared with a calendar, will also tell you if your event clashes with a race meeting in the area on that day or another big event that might clog the roads, take the public attention and jeopardise the success of yours.

As new ideas come up during preparations the chart will help you assess their potential within the overall strategy. You should also work into it check lists for each month with every detail you can think of, and have an arrangement for assessing the event *after* it has happened. This is important if you are to learn whether you have achieved your objectives and what should have been handled differently. The Billy Graham Crusades, for example, include planning for the following-up of converts through local churches as part of their very early advance meetings.

The flow chart is not supposed to be rigid or to be adhered to at all costs; more a source of guidance and reference and a way of keeping check on the different activities that go on simultaneously as you move towards that special day.

People are always niggling me and teasing me for doing too much work, going into too many details for even the smallest conference. But these same people always say, 'That ran like clockwork, Harvey' or 'What a great "do" that was, it looked terrific' and so on. They just don't make the connection!

Some people say you get tired and jaded with something if you plan too much or for too long. Wrong! Not with good strategic planning. Good planning gives you thinking time, the chance to anticipate problems and find ways of avoiding those stresses and crises that arise because you *haven't enough time to deal with the unexpected.*

Give it time

There are very few problems that cannot be overcome. The main reason they are not overcome is lack of *time* to discover the mistake and put it right.

It's a principle that applies to even the most straightforward things, like travel. It takes me half an hour to get from my home in North London to Heathrow Airport via the M25. That's on a good day. On a day of heavy traffic it could take an hour. I always leave a minimum of one and a half hours so that if I have a blow-out or breakdown or some other unforeseen emergency, I still have time to take care of it *and* catch the plane.

The result of this strategy is that I've never missed a plane in twenty-eight years of international travel - except once. That was in Frankfurt when a meeting over which I had no control went on just too long and I had no chance of making my flight. I caught the next one and as we arrived at Geneva we were told the flight before - the one I should have been on - had been blown up by a terrorist bomb. It was one of the first attacks and everyone on board had been killed.

Advancing

Much of the travelling I have done has been 'advancing', *the* vital part of effective event planning. It can be a long and weary job - especially if you've got more than one location - but there is no way to plan a conference, exhibition, rally or any other special event without proper advancing. Colleagues in politics and commerce still belittle my commitment to advance work. 'Surely you don't have to go there *again*,' they say, or 'Do you really need to take your assistant there *before* the start?' Yes, yes and yes again.

There is simply no substitute for knowing your venue (and how to get there) thoroughly. There is no other way of anticipating the potential and the problems or getting to know the local people you will need to solve them.

At one venue we were having two conferences three months

apart. Because the first one was quite small I did not give it the full 'advance' treatment that I usually do. I lived to regret it. We had crowd-flow blockages, insufficient refreshment facilities, no VIP entrance, no security check until people were in the main auditorium, and no way to get backstage except by walking right through the main meeting, up the stairs onto the stage and out through the back - with everybody watching! It caused us a lot of extra work, major changes and more travel to get it right for the second larger meeting.

From *The Longman Register of New Words*:

advance man *noun* someone who makes arrangements for visits and appearances by an eminent person, and goes in advance to ensure that they proceed smoothly.

Officially Mr Thomas is director of presentations for the Conservative party: unofficially he is the Prime Minister's personal advance man, as the current phrase goes. This is the year of the advance man. And when people say advance man, they usually mean Harvey Thomas.

Daily Telegraph 4 June 1987

▶ A word of US origin.

Thorough advancing is the heartfelt belief of a man who has worked in ninety-seven different countries. And travelled all the way round the world thirteen times. The military rightly say, 'Time spent on reconnaissance is never wasted'.

On my first visit to a venue I take photographs, get hold of the plans, make extensive notes - and there will still be a hundred things I'll miss. Like the fact that the plugs are the wrong size, or the electrical system is completely inadequate or, in the case of the Brighton Centre in 1988, that there are many different ceiling heights in the exhibition area! If you don't see and *feel* each event venue for yourself, you will not get the maximum potential out of it.

I would like to see the 'advance' man (or woman) used to much greater effect in this country. The Americans do it better. He should be brought in at the earliest stages to advise on venues – which would save time, money and frustration. He should be the link between the professionals at head office and the local knowledge of the on-the-spot workers.

He should have a say in how the guest speakers use their time at the event: should they meet the press or the mayor, where can they go for a bit of peace and quiet, even reassurance, and so on. The advance man will even be the person best qualified - from having sussed the location - to advise on menus, rehearsals and many other crucial details.

In so many areas the advance man (who may or may not be the same as the event organiser) has the on-the-spot knowledge which headquarters staff or the committee can never have - and it's a mistake not to get the maximum use from it.

The advance man knows the way to get VIPs in and out of the hall and how to manage their entrances and exits to the best effect. He also knows if a particular route will need clearing of cables, furniture and other obstacles. Ignorance of and unwillingness to accept the need for a good advance man causes more problems in event presentation than anything else.

Another of his tasks might be the gathering of voluntarily offered resources at the venue, whether it's free baize for the tables at a church fête, free mineral water or food from a local business, or the offer of cars to transport guests. The good advance man develops through experience the wisdom of knowing when to try something and when not. He has a sixth sense to recognise the genuine from the phoney.

I was the advance man for Mrs Thatcher in the 1987 General Election. When I arrived ten minutes before her at one stop (advance means a few minutes ahead as well as two months) I found that two ladies in wheelchairs had positioned themselves at the foot of the stairs and were pleading with everyone to let them stay and shake hands with Mrs Thatcher. Officials were trying to move them but after a word with our security people, we allowed them to stay.

It was a photo-opportunity for everyone but *only* because they genuinely wanted to be there, and to have their picture taken. That is the kind of occasion on which the advance man has to think fast, make a decision and 'manage' it through.

Something that he has to accept, however, is that there will be many, too many, occasions when great chunks of research or preparation are never used. You can spend an enormous amount of time checking out the possibilities for a particular audio-visual presentation only to find the organiser or speaker changes his mind. It's an occupational hazard.

In the Billy Graham team we had a saying 'But that was yesterday'. In the political world it's often 'But that was an hour ago'.

CHECK LIST

If your conference has a significant attendance, it may be worth your while to stage an exhibition and sell stands to related groups.

Here are some other staging considerations for you to think about.

Space	Facilities
square metres available	union position
open design - pillars?	porters
refreshment area	power supply
ceiling height(s)	water
lorry access	drainage
parking	lighting
height and width of doors	heating/cooling
storage space	storage
floor weight limits	decorating services
set-up time available	cleaning arrangements
relation to conference rooms	catering offered
cost	security

5
CHOOSING THE RIGHT PLACE

I appreciate your welcome.
As the cow said to the Maine farmer,
'Thank you for a warm hand on a cold morning.'
John F. Kennedy (Speech in Los Angeles, 1960)

Is that all of it?

The overview of the situation comes first.

When I was working in Australia I went swimming with some missionary friends near Darwin. We drove for miles through dense jungle and eventually came to a big pool which was maybe 150 metres square and 30 metres deep. I was a bit dubious at first, but I was hot and sticky and the water looked tempting. My friends and their little daughter went splashing blithely in so I threw caution to the winds and followed. We had a nice swim for half an hour or so.

As I climbed out I felt something tickling my toes. I looked down and saw a giant freshwater prawn almost a foot long. For someone used to the tiny creatures we get in England it was something of a shock and I said as much as I leapt into the air. 'Oh, that's nothing,' they said. 'This pool is filled with freshwater crocodiles and water pythons but they don't bother us so we didn't tell you.'

I said, 'If you'd told me that while I was in the pool, you'd have seen another miracle walking on the water!'

When you understand the whole picture your attitude towards it changes radically. I hadn't come to any grief by not having a comprehensive view of that crocodile pool, ignorance really was bliss that day; but when it comes to organising a major event, failure to see the overall picture *from the start* can blight the whole business. It is certainly crucial when it comes to choosing your venue.

We'll be talking about the important practical details you have to grapple with when making your selection, but the first and last point is always the overall view of the project and objectives. Why are we doing all this? What do we want to achieve? If you lose sight of *that*, all the attention to detail in the world is not a great deal of use.

Enjoy it

In Chapter Four I set out some of the reasons why conferences and other big events are held. I want to mention one here. It's often overlooked but it is probably the single most beneficial part - having a good time.

Now I'm not talking about a loud, wild time or a side-splitting, back-slapping drunken knees-up. I mean what the Bible calls 'the fellowshipping of yourselves together'. People want to enjoy the company of like-minded fellows. They like to renew old acquaintances, make new friends, see an interesting place in good company, recharge their batteries. They want to be *interested* and *happy*. But conference organisers and partici-pants often feel guilty about this aspect. They are nagged by the feeling that it's wrong to mix pleasure with business.

Business should be pleasure and politics should be fun!

That's realistic not frivolous. Nothing makes an impact in communication like enthusiastic personal contact. That's why we have conferences and rallies and congresses and debates and shows and exhibitions. Because they bring *people together*. Otherwise, we might as well all stay at home and stare at com-puter terminals.

Mark you, if the atmosphere at the venue is good, you can expand the outreach of your message a thousand times by television broadcast or closed circuit television relays to other venues. Look at the *Last Night of the Proms* from the Albert Hall; the whole country joins in. And the Wimbledon Final too. And if the nation is in need of a quiet sleep, we can all tune into cricket.

Venue personality

So, when you're picking the venue, remember that *atmosphere* will play a big part in your success. It will influence the reaction to the presentation and memories of it.

Some halls not only have no 'personality', but no potential for creating any. You learn to recognise them through experience; it's often an indefinable something that's lacking. More specifically, it may be the acoustics or the positioning of the seats or the stage, or it may be the 'coldness' of cement walls or the seediness of crumbling old ones.

The Bournemouth International Centre is an example of a place that lacks personality. The staff are great but, like many venues around the world, it was built for the architect's vision, not for practical multi-purpose use into the twenty-first century. The stage is tucked away like a box in the wall. There's no space over the top of it to 'fly' anything. An audience can only sit at the front of the stage and the hall stretches back for miles. There's nothing around the sides of the stage except cold brick walls and if you put anything there you cut down the already poor sight lines even more.

If they had accepted good professional *presentation* advice, they could have saved thousands, had a marvellous multi-purpose centre, proper crowd flow and huge potential for the next decade. I wonder why the right people are so rarely asked to help until it's too late?

Having said all that, there is usually something you can do to redeem a place. The Bournemouth International Centre is not really extensive or flexible enough for a modern Conservative Party Conference. However, because the management were helpful and co-operative we were able to make a few adjustments. We drained the swimming pool and turned the surrounds into a huge, light, warm, press area. We converted the kitchen into a production centre and extended the stage by three metres to make the sight lines passable and give us reasonable presentational potential.

DISTRACTED

Avoid venues with distracting views outside the windows - or pull the curtains!

I once had a half-day seminar in a conference room on the top floor of Chicago's O'Hare Hilton overlooking the O'Hare Airport runways, which crossed each other. By the end of the afternoon I was a nervous wreck. Chicago has the busiest airport in the world. Every few seconds a plane would take off as another approached the cross runway, with a third coming in behind the take-off plane to land. How they made it safely I will never know.

I never did find out what the seminar was about!

Bend it to what you want

It is always easier to create in a cavern than concoct in a corner.

If you have height and space you can do anything. Mrs Thatcher held her first rally for the European Elections at the National Exhibition Centre in Birmingham - Hall 6. It is a great barn of a place which seats 5,000 but which that day was due to hold 2,500. So we had to shrink the hall.

We put up 6m muffle boards two-thirds of the way back, erected a four-row tiered seating block in front of them and built a 24m by 11m stage at the front. We 'flew' huge flags and posters one metre in from the side walls, reaching to some two metres above the ground. A big backdrop to the stage with light concentrated on it did the rest. We even had space for a refreshment area behind the muffle boards at the back of the hall. A powerful organ added the final touches with lively and popular 'European' music.

The fact that Hall 6 is a bare cavern with iron girders didn't matter at all by the time we had finished. We had created a colourful, well-lit, attractive, atmospheric setting out of virtually nothing.

For a bigger event, it is always better to go for an empty

room that allows you scope to do your own thing rather than a place which has limiting fixed features. That's why, for instance, it's easier to produce a big conference at the Brighton Conference Centre where there is almost austere simplicity than it is in Blackpool's charming but inflexible Winter Gardens. The atmosphere we create is *different* but not better or worse in either Brighton or Blackpool.

One of the best major centres I have worked or seen is the International Congress Centre in Berlin, which has two auditoria with a stage in the middle. This arrangement is so flexible it can be used for anything from tennis to *Holiday on Ice* to huge international congresses and exhibitions.

Your venue provides the actual meeting room or hall *and* all your ancillary needs, food, exhibitions, office space etc. Let me, for a moment, concentrate on the meeting room alone.

The main auditorium

Although you *can* shrink a hall by various techniques, it is not ideal. What you want is a location that is always comfortably filled. This is the rule for bigger conferences - two hundred people or more - because these are more the 'show' conferences.

If you are going to reach people through the media, *never* have many empty seats. It looks bad. Have the place filled and a few people standing. This needs careful organising! On the last afternoon - are many people leaving? Then move some chairs out and spread the others.

Before you confirm a venue, plan your strategy for seat occupation in the main hall.

At the CBI Initiative 1992 Press Launch in October 1988, we used the Methven Room at Centre Point in London. There were 220 chairs. The CBI team estimated a total attendance of 120 (they were exactly right). A hundred chairs 'disappeared', the rows became a little more spacious, aisles were one seat wider, space was left for photographers - and the press conference was packed, creating the vital 'success' atmosphere to set the tone to launch an important strategic project.

When you choose your meeting room, the size has to be such that there always *appears* to be more interest in the event than the organisers anticipated. This generates atmosphere and publicity if you are looking for it.

I learned this principle in the first big event I was involved in: Billy Graham's Crusade at Maine Road Stadium in Manchester in 1961. For nearly thirty years that crusade has been regarded as one of his least successful, whereas a later British Crusade at Earls Court in London in 1966 has always been seen as a triumph.

An average of 35,000 people a night attended Maine Road; only 22,000 a night attended Earls Court - a third less. *But* Earls Court only holds 20,000 and Maine Road football stadium had a capacity of 50,000, so people looking at the crowds at Manchester always saw one empty or thinly populated stand. Earls Court, on the other hand, was so packed we had to use overflow rooms. (Moral: perceived success is what goes into the history books, not actual success.)

The size of the venue, therefore, is one of your first considerations and it might be helpful here to divide conferences into two types: open and closed. These divisions influence all considerations in choosing your venue: accessibility, flexibility and presentational potential, facilities, crowd flow and that indefinable something - 'charisma'.

A *closed* conference is for purely private discussion which neither wants nor needs publicity. The other kind, the *open* conference or public event, does. You want the world to see what's going on and must therefore attract the press and even radio and television.

Getting the right size of meeting place is always a priority. You have to ensure that everyone is comfortable, that there is space between rows, at the front and down the aisles. Over-crowding distracts as much as empty seats. Plan room to 'breathe' and have space you can move into - even if it's only a corridor where you have coffee - that gives your audience and the room a break.

Can we help you?

There are far too many places advertising 'conference facilities' that offer nothing more than rooms of different sizes. Stay away from them. However small your event is, don't hold it in a hotel or other venue that does not provide good crowd flow, catering service, easy-to-reach toilets and any other facilities you need. There are enough good venues around - starve the poor ones of your business. It is achieving your objective that matters, not 'We always go to the Knot and Muddle.'

Flexibility and presentational potential are important too. Is the management of your venue adaptable enough to cope with changes in your programme or its timing? This might be the tiniest thing but if it is wrongly handled, it will inconvenience everyone and leave an uneasy or even bad memory. Suppose you've scheduled your meetings till 12.30 but you get through the morning's business more quickly than you expected. Are the hotel or centre staff going to throw up their arms in horror if you want an earlier lunch so that you can press on with the afternoon session?

Before you commit to a venue go there yourself and find out what exactly it will provide and what the extras will be. Can they offer you any exclusive services or facilities?

For instance: are the soft drinks in the conference sessions free; do you pay for meals actually eaten or expected numbers; are the hotel's public address system and audio-visual facilities adequate and available without charge; do they provide electricity and power for extra lighting free?

Most conference venues fall down on the little matters of personal caring. There aren't enough biscuits; you can have tea and coffee in the morning but only tea in the afternoon; no-one knows where the switches are or how the equipment works; and so on. The impression you get is that no individual is taking care of *your* particular conference. This attitude reflects badly on the conference service industry and demonstrates that it has still not fully come to terms with the need for quality and a caring approach in its business.

The head of a training department for a big bank in the City of London recently asked me if I could help find him suitable conference locations. We checked out hundreds of hotels but only found thirty-five or forty that met the basic-facilities criteria. He wanted to set up seventy-five gatherings a year!

The CBI Initiative 1992 held ten seminars for 150 people each, in thirteen centres all over the country. The venues were hard to find.

The Americans plan things better. European conference venues suffer from chronic diseases: small doors, narrow stairs, no lifts at all or tiny lifts added to the building as an afterthought, poor electrics, low ceilings, 'miles away' kitchens, staff curfews, meaningless rules and no ramps.

Avoid Mr Jobsworth! The man who says when you need a door opened to save a long walk - 'It's more than my jobsworth, mate'.

FIRST-CLASS HOTELS

For a really good example of a venue I must point to Washington DC and either the Sheraton/Shoreham hotels (individually or as a combination) or the Washington Hilton.

The Hilton's ballroom is a classic model of flexible facilities. It holds between 3,000 and 4,000 altogether, but it can also be divided up by electronically controlled walls to give one area of half its size and two quarter areas. The soundproofing between its three sections is excellent and helped enormously by the fact that the PA system drops sound down from the ceiling rather than pushing it out from the front. You can have three choirs singing their heads off in the separate sections without any of them disturbing the other.

The Sheraton and Omni Shoreham hotels can cope with 5,000 delegates comfortably. Forty 'syndicate' rooms with full technical and catering services can accommodate forty to 200 people at a banquet, and more if theatre-style seating is used.

Crowd flow in these three locations is so good that non-conference guests can stay there during even the largest event without inconvenience.

Hotels that do offer good professional facilities with personal service and attention to detail are sadly still few and far between. There is huge unexplored potential in this field. Conferences and other such events are not going to go away.

'May I present . . .'

The presentational aspect involves all kinds of different considerations which I shall come to presently, but what they boil down to is this: what can you do to make it easier for the communicator to communicate and the audience to receive the required message - with *minimum* distraction?

'No distraction' is always the priority, but more so at a large event. At small conferences people tend to be in the mood to concentrate. At larger ones, you have to work harder to grab and hold their attention.

On the other hand, some problems show up more markedly at smaller gatherings. For example, if you have sudden feedback with a microphone which produces a dreadful screech, 5,000 people will just laugh. It's more likely to throw everyone off course if it happens in a little room with a small audience. With bigger groups the atmosphere takes over and helps combat the hitches. Smaller gatherings are more personal and the mess-ups actually stand out more, and are more likely to happen.

Similarly in smaller conferences, shabbiness and tattiness of surroundings stick out more; everyone is closer to them. Perhaps the most noticeable factors here are cleanliness and light. You don't want grotty curtains, draughts, windows that won't close or open properly, obvious holes in the carpet or old air-conditioning that is too noisy.

Check out the seating arrangements, platform or stage (if there is one) and its relation to the main entrance. Speakers are handicapped when the main entrance doors are behind them and every time they open, the audience's eyes swivel in that direction and attention is gone. Also check audio-visual aids, the PA system, ceiling heights, flooring, size of access doors and sight lines.

Unless you have a very small conference of less than a

hundred people avoid low ceilings; it's like being in a crowded rail commuter carriage and everyone feels oppressed and claustrophobic. I've worked in a number of centres where the fire alarm has been set off by the heat from our lights. In one place a television 'red head' (800 watt) light set off the sprinkler system with hysterical results. You'd better know the theory and the practice of the venue's fire regulations. (Some centres require all seats to be linked together; in others you have more layout leeway.)

'Make room there . . .'

A good venue should have high and wide goods access doors - at least 3.5m high. Sets for exhibitions and conferences these days can be large, complicated and costly. It's no use having a fantastic set if you can't get it into the building. Attempts to squeeze in through too small openings inevitably result in Laurel and Hardy-style disasters - try taking a 3m panel into the Barbican in London!

For any serious exhibition or conference you need commercial goods lifts. 'Flow' for the building materials should have no sharp corners, narrow passages or stairs. Look for ramps, wide passages and large loading doors. If you can drive an articulated truck to the main floor from the street outside, you know you're in business. (That's a good point at the Bournemouth International Centre!)

Be specific in checking out a venue's own audio-visual equipment. If you know your speaker wants an overhead projector, make sure they've got one that works. If you're going to use slides, see that the room can be darkened easily - and check your sightlines.

Visibility is a key factor in any event whether it's seeing who's opening the church fête or watching a celebrity sing. Look at how the stage is positioned and its depth, or whether there are pillars or any other view-blockers. Sightlines can be a good reason for choosing a clear open hall where you can build your own platform or stage. The principle applies even with very small conferences.

A constant bane of the conference organiser is arriving at a venue to load and unload a dozen mini computers, audio-visual equipment, tape recorders, packets of paper and the like, six or eight times onto trolleys, carrying them up or down steps, grazing elbows squeezing into lifts or staggering miles under their weight - all before arriving at the place where they have to be set up. Not to mention the bumps and bruises on the centre's staff going the opposite way in a hurry.

Make life as easy as possible for yourself by picking a venue with good access for sets and materials.

Floors

When it comes to flooring, I never fail to be amazed at the lack of consultation with the professionals when a new centre is being planned. One of the many frequent hazards in this business, be it syndicate rooms or stadia, is the floor surface. The Germans do this better than most: Frankfurt airport has a synthetic studded floor which is now widely imitated. It's quiet, safe and looks good.

The Americans go for the 'slippery when wet' floors and it's amazing how often floors can get wet!

If you're faced with a slippery floor problem, it is inexpensive these days to get exhibition contractors to supply some cheap carpeting and you may want to investigate this option. It can be money well spent making the place smarter and safer.

'Can you see?'

A good presenter can create an atmosphere in an empty room or hall. The problems usually lie not with emptiness, which can be filled, but with the fixed building created by a designer who thought he was being terribly clever but whose design has hindered events ever since.

If you find yourself offered a standard layout of chairs, don't be afraid to try something different. Changing things gives you the initiative. At one TV training session I swapped the whole room around, putting the audience on the stage and doing the presentation from the floor! They saw better and I had more space to work in; but no-one had thought of it before.

Good sight lines are more important than evenness of chair layout. Most organisers set them rigidly in straight rows without checking whether some other design might give everyone a better view and provide more working and movement space.

Moving the people

Now then - crowd flow! Movement of people. It's important in small conferences where there are limited numbers moving slowly, but for bigger events it's absolutely crucial. The answer is to make the crowd flow *through*, not in and back out again.

When people are moving in all directions, meeting dead ends and trying to push back to the start, it's not only chaotic, it's downright dangerous. It can also be a security headache. Think of a conference as an aircraft: it needs air flowing over its wings to give it lift.

So you need more than 'just enough' space - in corridors, past exhibition stands, into and out of the main forum, to the toilets and refreshment facilities; more than theory or the fire inspector demands. Think in terms of *ease* more than *possibility*, of movement for the number of people you anticipate. When in doubt, leave more space rather than less.

In conferences our movement problems have, for the most part, been caused by a 'political' insistence on cramming more chairs, more people into inadequate space, including the stage. For some reason my clients nearly always ask: 'Where can we put more people?' Rarely: 'What is the right way of achieving our objectives? What would the best venue be?'

Work out ways of splitting the incoming crowd and directing them where you want them to go. That alone would have avoided the Hillsborough football crowd disaster in 1989. Make plenty of clear, highly visible signs, maps even if the venue is large enough to warrant it. Put firm barriers where you don't want people to go and have enough stewards and security men to help. Find people who will do the job well - don't pick them just because they are there.

If you do muddle up the crowd-flow arrangements, over-stretch the facilities or pick an unsuitable venue in the first place, you cause enormous distractions *from the event* and *the message*. The participants feel flustered, uncomfortable, annoyed and unlikely to want to come again next time.

There are certainly no more rats in the Isle of Man than anywhere else. It seems though that they handle them better. On a recent visit we learned of a 'rat run' from nests down to the stream - through hedges, across the road, all well established. A new building project however wrecked a portion of the 'run'. The rats, in a panic on the first night, hit the barricade and swarmed everywhere, including some spots where they were definitely not welcome. Any similarity to people is entirely co-incidental!

'How do I get there?'

I've left the question of accessibility of the venue until last, not because it's less important but because it's one of the most important considerations and impinges on one of the most difficult tasks any event organiser has to face: getting the right number of the right people to come to it. 'Bottoms on seats.'

Effective marketing, the programme offered, the speakers appearing, the styles of presentation - all these elements contribute to pulling in the public and the theme of 'bottoms on seats' will appear again as I deal with them. But it's something you must think about right from the start when you're choosing your venue.

Unless you want to hire coaches and bus people in (not unknown) you must pick a place people will be able to get to fairly easily. Accessibility is not so important with the small, closed conferences because the participants are usually either highly motivated in the first place (because of specialist interest or commitment) or their employers require them to go or at least agree that they should. So they can come with time off work and probably on an expense account, even to a far-flung location.

With the larger events, however, the net has to be cast

wider and an individual's decision on whether to attend will undoubtedly be influenced by the convenience factor.

Amateur organisers inevitably pick a venue for the wrong reasons. It's the 'turn' of a particular hotel or city, or they choose it because they have a vague idea that it might be rather nice to go to Torquay next year, or even - worst of all - because 'We've always had it there'!

When the *motives* are wrong the venue is nearly always far less than the best.

A good organiser is totally objective, even downright hard-hearted in choosing venue, style, speakers and programme. Look at the people you're trying to reach. What money will they have to spend on a trip? How far will they have to travel? Will the event be worth it to them?

You can hardly expect people to make a journey of six hours round trip for an afternoon's event unless it is very special. How near is your proposed venue to airports (if it involves international visitors), and the road and rail links. It might be great to have something in Torquay if you're hoping to draw visitors from the southwest, but not if you're trying to pull a big public audience from Tyneside.

Don't eliminate somewhere because it sounds ridiculous or out of the question. In these days of competitive air fares many overseas locations can be as cost effective as being in the UK.

In setting up big rallies in Berlin's Olympic Stadium in 1981, we had two committee members in London (my wife Marlies and me), two in Berlin and two in the United States (living in Virginia Beach and Los Angeles). We found that it was cheaper for the four Europeans to travel to America than for the two Americans to come to London or Berlin. So once each month from June 1980 until June 1981, Marlies and I rushed out to Heathrow Airport early Friday afternoon, flew to North America (Toronto, Washington DC, Los Angeles, Virginia Beach, etc) and worked in committee through Saturday. Sunday morning we preached at different churches and flew back to London over Sunday night, to bounce cheerily into the office on Monday morning. Amazingly we saved thousands of pounds that way!

Also remember that accessibility considerations apply to the media if you want to attract them. They not only have to be able to get there but they have to be able to get their words and pictures *out*. This does not mean 'just-enough' telecommunications on site; it may also mean the nearness to a micro-wave or satellite TV link or surface links to a major town.

For quiet study conferences, remote old-fashioned, ill-equipped venues in places like Scarborough and Buxton might be great. But, please, *not* for twentieth century media conferences.

Finally, go to the place *yourself*. I know this sounds obvious but it's surprising how many organisers depend on brochures, models and plans (it's fine to have those as well, of course) or even their recollections of a place five years ago (when it and your needs were different). Strike up some personal rapport with the person in charge of the centre so that he or she is more likely to go that extra mile for you. Make sure they know what's really going on in your mind, and what your objectives are.

PET 'HOTEL HATES' (THE FREQUENT ONES)

- narrow stairs and no lifts
- low shower pressure
- telephone kiosks built for left-handed midgets
- only one plug, down on the floor under the bed and 5AMP
- hairdryers on 1m fixed lead from the floor socket 3m away from wall mirror facing opposite direction
- just two 40 watt lamps to read and work by
- toilet rolls positioned for contortionists only
- room service that brings each course separately throughout *Dallas*
- radiators that haven't been on for years
- radiators that won't go off
- basins that take half an hour to empty after you've cleaned your teeth and you want to shave
- stoppers that hang under the cold water tap but don't reach the drain
- stoppers that have no chain so you wallow in the dirty water to find them
- toilets where you can sit down or close the door but not both

---

The venue staff should be able to demonstrate all their equipment and facilities, and understand your technical requests. Watch out for the 'Oh the electrician will be here on the day - I'm sure' syndrome. He won't!

And beware of those who want to take over the organiser's job. Frequently venue staff try to set everything up before you arrive, on the basis that it worked for the people before you and it's less effort for them. No two conferences are ever the same. You and the venue manager need to make the arrangements together. Put them in writing and be sure you know and he understands what you want to achieve.

6
WHAT'S ON?

It is far more difficult to be simple
than to be complicated

John Ruskin

Does it contribute?

When you've set your objectives, sorted out the budget, chosen the venue and fixed the date, the next step is to plan the programme. Again, it's of paramount importance to keep an overview so that you can gear each aspect towards achieving the objective. If you don't know what you want to do, you can never judge whether you've done it.

Remember: to achieve your objective you need to interest, inform and involve.

You get the interest by inviting good speakers to talk on the right subjects and by your format variety and, wherever possible, the right kind of sparkle.

You inform by making sure that the programme is not just froth and bubble, that it has genuine body.

And you involve by making sure you draw the required visible response from the audience.

So the question is not 'What (who) shall we have in the programme?' - but 'What programme must I have to achieve my objectives?'

Too often people throw up ideas - 'Let's have so-and-so as a speaker on Tuesday and a dance on the Wednesday and a banquet on Thursday' - without ever stopping to think how any of these will help reach goals or fit into the overall time. They make these suggestions because, 'Well, that's what people do at conferences, isn't it?' The ideas might be splendid in themselves but you must consider how they will contribute to the strategy.

Do you, for instance, want a disco because it will bring a welcome break to an otherwise (necessarily) heavy and demanding programme, or could it prove *too* sharp a contrast and interrupt the concentration you're trying to establish? Is a banquet going to make everyone feel pleasantly pampered or is it going to cause hangovers and indigestion the next morning when you've got some crucial business to get through?

I can't decide for you, but don't ignore the questions; consider the pros and cons and then decide. A programme is not just what happens in the conference hall. It covers every aspect of the entire time that participants are present in the city or town where it's being held.

Start with the free time

When you plan your programme, start with the social and personal free time for shopping or relaxation that the participants ought to have to encourage their brains to work during the meaty sessions. Don't compromise that free time. If you do, the participants will play truant anyway - probably at the wrong times!

This goes back to what I was saying about the 'fellowship' of conferences and similar events and how important it is for people to enjoy themselves and make contacts. They ought to get to know each other, see a little of the place they are in, have time to shop for family souvenirs and sample the local food and culture. If you try to squeeze these requirements in around the mainstream business, you will be left with scrappy little bits of free time that are useless, and your visitors will feel cheated.

So you *start* by saying (and these are purely arbitrary divisions, you can work out your own): 'We're here for three nights and four days, let's have one evening completely free, two or three meals in different, interesting locations (include transport time) and perhaps half a day free for shopping.' Mark that time on the schedule and regard it as sacrosanct. What you're left with then is the time for the 'meat' of the programme. That way, you will ensure that people will be pleased - they all want free time - and the programme doesn't suffer.

Stagger the time

A programme does not have to be conventionally 'nine to five' structured but participants are more likely to accommodate themselves to unusual arrangements if you've given them time for themselves. So if you would usually start the programme with the address from the mayor at 9.30am, consider having the mayor speak at a breakfast at 8am and then give everyone a two-hour break from 11am to have a sight-seeing walk or shopping session before returning for lunch. Alternatively, have a lengthy 'heavy' morning session and a free afternoon, perhaps with optional social events for those who want them.

You might then have a working dinner with a business speaker. It's the basic principle of presentation: almost anything works well as long as you do it deliberately and explain it clearly and pleasantly, and make it interesting.

GOOD PROGRAMMING

The 1989 National Religious Broadcasters Convention in Washington was a first rate example of balanced and varied programming.

It lasted three days and during that time the 4,000 delegates had a choice of plenary sessions with top speakers, technical study groups, workshops, banquets, free time and even great music. The theme of the convention was carried through by every speaker and in every session.

Since attendance at everything was voluntary there was plenty of time to view the high-tech exhibition and to mingle and chat in any of the dozens of coffee shops on the site. Video and audio cassettes of each session were available at the bookshop within twenty minutes of the finish, which is the time when people want to buy them.

Another good feature was the sponsored breakfasts each morning at 7am: they saved delegates expense and guaranteed a good turn out.

Setting the tone

Every element contributes to the whole. Of course, you will be enthusiastic when you're planning a programme. The trouble starts when people get carried away. They say, 'Why don't we show this great movie one evening?' without considering how this 'great movie' contributes. One man's job was to select films for airlines and cruise ships. He lasted a week until he supplied *Flight 219 Mayday* to an airline and *The Poseidon Adventure* to a liner.

When you select an item for a programme, consider how it will contribute to your goal and how it could affect mood and outlook. Be sure of the strategy before you embark on the mechanics. Maximum 'razzamatazz' is not always right and sometimes it can be counter-productive.

Suppose you are having a conference for your sales people to tell them about a new product. You will find that a good audio-visual presentation and some agreeable refreshments afterwards are all you need for them to welcome the information and instruction. If you want to motivate them to go out and sell that product, you've got to make them feel it is important to them. You want them to exert their self-discipline and use their talents in your favour. So you really don't want a situation where they go out and get drunk every night. Catch their interest and spark their enthusiasm so that they begin to see the product's potential. How something that is good for the company will be good for them. How it will earn them more money.

The 'programme' for your event covers the whole period the participants are present in the city. It includes handling their reception at the station, airport or parking lot. First impressions last. Each detail must be designed to help create the right response, the desired mood - to bring you another step nearer towards achieving your goals.

If you are running a rally aimed at inspiring and motivating people, don't start by having them arrive in a strange city to find the car park full, the nearest suitable alternative two miles away and no taxis available because it's Sunday evening and pouring with rain. You probably can't do much about the rain, but you can work out contingency plans such as having helpers to park participants' cars or arranging minibuses to shuttle between the centre and the car park.

Sometimes you can turn what at first seems a mess into a

triumph, with a little imagination.

For instance, at the Conservative Party Conference in Brighton in 1988, we had to turn the building 'back to front' for security reasons and have the main entrance at the rear. People arriving at the car park or taxi set-down point had a four or five minute walk to the main entrance, which was through the ground floor of a multi-storey car park.

We appointed some friendly stewards whose sole job was to encourage people from their point of arrival to their destination. They gave information and made conversation. We couldn't shorten the walk, but we made people *feel* better about it. When the participants finally reached the multi-storey car park, they found a pleasant white-walled entrance hall with a blue muslin ceiling, nicely decorated with flags and Party symbols and brightly lit. You see, it's not up to the participants to come in the right mood. It is up to you to put them in the mood you want.

Make them feel looked after. When they get to the hotel have someone to greet them, someone who knows names, and can help with transport, luggage, the pre-registration formalities. Provide a (decent-looking) security pass and all the necessary care and attention to make the participants feel welcome, comfortable and enthusiastic about what is going to happen next. That way, the conference gets off to a good start because people are raring to go and in the right frame of mind. And if conference participants see that your organisation is well-run and thoughtful, they are more likely to respond as you want them to.

This same feeling should be carried into the first welcome meeting which should set the tone in the way that gospel singer George Beverly Shea did for Billy Graham. It was Petula Clark who set the feeling at the first rally for Mrs Thatcher after she became Prime Minister. Her version (slightly rewritten for the occasion) of 'This is My Song' brought the house down and everyone was ready to listen to the main speech.

Your guests, your audience, your congregation need to feel part of what's happening. They need to know where you're taking them. Give them that outline, the feeling of involvement and purpose, at the opening session. The delegate arriving to an indifferent reception or lack of clear information, even a misspelt name, soon starts to believe that he's dealing with incompetents. He wishes he were back home. He may feel he's in a British Rail nightmare: he will get to his destination some time or other but he's deeply unhappy about his discomfort while travelling.

I'm reminded of the story about the time when a British Rail advertising contract was up for grabs. It was a huge budget and the top agencies were eager to get their hands on it. It was prestigious, lucrative and a creative challenge. The agencies laid on the works: marvellous hospitality, slick presentation, sophisticated arguments. All except one. That one invited the railway VIPs to their office to see and hear their sales pitch as the others had done.

When the big wigs arrived, however, they were barely acknowledged by a dour receptionist, told to sit in a grubby waiting area strewn with cigarette ends and empty coffee cups, and kept waiting for half an hour without either apology or explanation. Just as they were about to explode with rage the head of the agency appeared. 'Gentlemen,' he said. 'Now you know how the average rail customer feels.' He got the contract.

One embarrassing experience involved Jan Leeming, the television personality, who was taking part in a film I was producing. Unfortunately no-one had been able to see her accommodation beforehand and we found that the hotel she had been booked into was a nightmare - tatty rooms with cigarette burns, door handles which fell off, threadbare carpets. A colleague made cheerful conversation with Jan while another of the team hurriedly arranged a better room. Actually, Jan is a very sweet lady and a good professional and she would happily have stayed in that room - but it would have been wrong.

Apply the principles: check it out ahead of time and put yourself in the other person's place. There is an old Sioux saying: 'You cannot understand a man until you have walked two weeks in his moccasins.'

Strictly speaking these things fall outside what most people think of as 'the programme'. They are just as important though as what goes on in the main body of the conference centre. It's your attitude to people which wins them over.

The programme jigsaw

A conference is a bit like a jigsaw, the participants, debates, guest appearances, audio-visual presentations, workshops, free and social time - they all have to click together to provide the complete picture. When you come to detailed programme planning, you need variety and balance and, if you have a great deal to get through and a concentrated message to communicate, you still have to break it up and give people a chance to relax their brains as well as their bodies.

Every programme needs highlights. There's only one FA Cup Final, one Wimbledon, one Royal Ascot every season, even though there's plenty of football, tennis and racing at other times. If you provide memorable highlights, people will go away feeling the whole event was good; they will gradually forget the weak parts of the event (though I hope *you* won't).

People today are used to getting their information in small doses: a newspaper paragraph, a news item on television. They have short attention spans so don't expect them to sit for hours on end without fidgeting, yawning or falling asleep. As I said in an earlier chapter, the principle of speaking is not to go on for more than a few minutes without getting your audience to do *something* - applaud or laugh or raise their hands. The same principle applies with conference programmes.

To get maximum impact, break up the messages and the format. Skilful, experienced speakers will do this themselves. If you have inexperienced speakers, curtail their time. Vary the programme with humour, audio-visual devices, music, movement, colour, question and answer sessions, guest appearances.

You want your audience to be active, not passive. You want them to respond, rather like the vicar who 'wired-up' his pews. It was a novel method of fund-raising. 'Who'll give £25?' he asked and pressed a button. Several leapt to their feet. 'Alleluia,' he replied. 'And who'll give me £50?' Another button - dozens more responded. 'Praise the Lord', said the vicar. 'And now £100?' Another button and up stood the rest. 'How did your appeal go?' a colleague asked later. 'Great,' came the reply, 'except for one Scotsman who was electrocuted.' Perhaps a little too active but he did achieve his goal!

Food at last

Mealtimes provide natural variation in a programme and what you are going to offer will depend on the programme, the venue's facilities, the season, the numbers and your budget. My advice here is to avoid a lot of fancy twiddly bits - unless you're running a conference for French gourmets.

Most people prefer something simple and easy to eat. They will be talking as they eat and it's distracting and embarrassing to have to juggle something fussy and awkward while you're trying to make new friends and business contacts. Bangers and mash is better than pretentious *nouvelle cuisine*, though you can probably be a little more original!

The food in the hospitality rooms at the Republican Party's National Convention in Dallas in 1984 was particularly good. They had huge piles of chilled fresh pineapple and other fresh fruits and cheeses all beautifully arranged and cut up into bite-sized pieces. The quality was superb. No-one had to worry about plates and forks. We all went home having had little but fruit, cheese and Texas-size shrimps for three days, but it was delicious, convenient and appealing, and there was plenty of it.

Drawing the people

Last but certainly not least, when you're planning your programme, remember the hardest single task in a conference is getting people to come to it. In-house or company conferences have a ready-made audience and your main consideration is getting the right mix of personnel, senior management, middle management and so forth. But for larger events you have to 'sell' them - metaphorically if not literally.

Decide who you want to attend, where they are, how

they will get to you and what will appeal to them. There are heavy demands on people's time these days and a lot of rival attractions. Sometimes, particularly where you have a specific audience, the task may be primarily a logistical one - moving them from A to B - and you can solve this by bussing them in.

When your potential catchment is broader based you have to find additional ways of drawing them in. An obvious method is to advertise but be careful that you aim the right kind of advertising in the right direction, otherwise it is money badly spent. The Billy Graham organisation used to estimate that only ten per cent of their crowds came as a direct result of advertising and, generally speaking, I find that *by itself* it is the least cost-effective way of marketing events; the most effective being personal invitation.

Most significant things, from marriages to murders, happen between people who know each other well, so the best way to reach people is by word of mouth in the right places. Start with the stalwarts of the organisation and let the message fan out from there, snowballing as it goes along. All the advertising in the world will not draw people to your event if they believe they're going to be there alone. Let them know it's going to have a fabulous programme and be full of people they know or others of a like mind. That's when they get interested.

When we were setting up Eurofest '75 - an evangelistic congress for 8,000 young people in Brussels in 1975 - a number of advertising agents came to 'sell' me on their company. Forty-seven countries were involved, so they had dreams of a big account. One girl was a hard, chain-smoking sales machine letting me know I could not set up a multi-national congress without multi-national advertising. I asked if she had ever been to hear Billy Graham; a bit unlikely I thought. 'Oh yes,' she said, 'I heard him once.' 'What on earth got you to go?' I asked. 'Oh,' she said, 'a friend came round and asked me to go with her . . . Ah, I see what you mean.' We got 2,000 reps in forty-seven countries who averaged four recruits each!

And if you want 70,000 people at a birthday tribute concert for Nelson Mandela, you push the information through to organisations like CND, The World Council of Churches, and you'll have a full house!

In an emergency you can, of course, also try straightforward 'bribery', depending on how much you want to spend: free meals, free accommodation, free transport etc. On the other hand, you might appeal to their finer feelings, their sense of duty and responsibility. With a political party, for example, this might mean conveying the idea that the Foreign Secretary is making an important speech in their locality and they owe it to him to show their support.

But professionally, you can do much of it with your programme. You create an interest by having appealing people to speak, by arranging debates that will be gripping, even controversial, by having one or more celebrities present, by asking a well-known band to perform, by offering special food, by spectacle, by drama, by electronic presentations. The list is long and varied and what you choose or the combinations you try will depend on what you want your event to achieve.

The bigger the event, the harder you will have to work at crowd-pulling and the earlier you will have to start to build up the interest.

NATIONAL PRAYER BREAKFAST

The National Prayer Breakfast in the United States is an annual gathering of political and religious leaders and other key national figures who meet to pray for the nation. This was the programme for the 1989 meeting.

Pre-breakfast prayer: The Honourable Charles Grassley, US Senator, Iowa

Opening song: US Naval Academy Chapel Choir (in uniform)

Presiding: The Honourable Bob Stump, US Representative, Arizona

Opening prayer: General Larry D. Welch, Chief of Staff, US Air Force

Breakfast: chilled fresh orange juice, Cheddar omelette, O'Brien potatoes, chutney-filled peach, croissants and apple spice muffins, butter and fruit preserves, tea, coffee and brewed decaffeinated coffee.

Message from the United States Senate: The Honourable Paul Simon, US Senator, Illinois

Old Testament reading: The Honourable John Buchanan, Premier of Nova Scotia, Canada

New Testament reading: Art Monk, all-pro wide receiver, Washington Redskins.

Solo: Sandi Patti

Message from United States Congress: The Honourable Ike Skelton, US Representative, Missouri

Reading: Justice Sandra Day O'Connor, US Supreme Court

Prayer for national leaders: Dr Billy Graham

Message: The Honourable Alan Simpson, US Senator, Wyoming

The President of the United States

Closing song: Sandi Patti

Closing prayer: Mrs Susan Baker.

Now that's what I call a programme. It lasted only one and a half hours but it satisfied body and soul.

7
HAVE STAPLE GUN - WILL TRAVEL

If you can keep your head when all about you
Are losing theirs and blaming it on you
Rudyard Kipling

Right, you've worked out your budget, you've chosen your venue and you've planned the most marvellous programme that will pack 'em in. Now, you've got to get down to the real nitty gritty: how will the stage look, what about the sound system, who presses what buttons for the audio-visuals and when . . .?

This chapter is about details but, as usual, the same principles still apply: have your overall picture and your ultimate objective in mind and aim to make it easy for the presenter to present and audience to receive.

Sticky tape and live wires

When people walk into an auditorium, one thing ought to happen and another ought not: their attention should be grabbed and held but at the same time they shouldn't fall flat on their faces because you've failed to gaffer down a loose wire.

This is hands-on conference presentation, a case of 'have staple gun, will travel'. You might not exactly be able to pack up all your troubles in an old kit bag, but if your rally bag isn't packed you *will* have trouble.

Gaffer tape, for instance – an all-purpose cloth tape that sticks to any surface but is easy to remove. It is strong and non-damaging and is probably the one absolutely essential piece of equipment you need above all others. Don't, as they say, leave home without it. Most people in this business opt for two-inch wide tape but I prefer three-inch black for securing every line of wire in the hall, plus some two-inch white or silver to mark the edge of steps and other things you need to make noticeable. Three-inch gaffer is not common, but you can get it if you hunt around.

(Bitter experience has taught me to remove the gaffer at the end of the event *only* by holding the wire down on the floor as you pull the tape up. If you don't hold the wire on the floor, the tape will wrap itself round it and you'll have a terrible time trying to disentangle the resulting blob of sticky goo.)

You also need lots of electrical extension leads and bars of four 13 amp sockets. Fuses blow from the amount of *power* used, not the number of sockets.

Light and heat use power. Virtually nothing else uses very much. Thus you can run thirty electric typewriters off one 13 amp socket but only three 800 watt lamps. A simple formula to calculate the amps is to divide the watts (usually marked on the bottom of the appliance) by the volts: the result is amps. You can pull around 3,000 watts off one 13 amp socket.

So with videos, word processors and so on, life is easy. Bring in a few television lamps though and watch your amps. Are there electricians on site? - preferably *not* the night porter who *says* he 'knows how it works'.

The first rule of safety is never to have electrical wires *off the ground*, and gaffer everything on the ground. The second is never to leave on the floor a *closed loop* of wire or string. A closed loop that someone can catch their foot in and trip is one of the most frequent causes of industrial accidents. In Covent Garden Market every band from every box of fruit, vegetables and flowers is cut.

The third rule is to wear hard-soled and protective shoes whenever you are setting up. At an election rally in the Wembley Conference Centre in 1983, I stood on a nail in my training shoes and it went nearly four centimetres into my foot.

Apart from not actually having members of your audience fall headlong, the other main consideration when getting them into and out of their seats is ease of movement. Organisers are frequently met with what appears to be rigid rules - 'We always have a five foot aisle, sir, it's all we need' - when in fact the reality should be far more flexible, better suited to your particular needs and safer too.

Focusing on the platform

The main focus of your audience's attention will be the backdrop and the stage, and, on or near it, the audio-visual point and the speaking lectern.

First though, one of my bugbears: people on the platform. In theory, the platform is for those actually taking part in the programme. In practice, the platform becomes a place for people who want to be seen, those who believe that their own importance is such that the presentation of the programme is secondary to their right to be seen beside the programme participants.

This leads to a definite conflict of interests - yours and theirs! In principle, platform numbers should be kept to an absolute minimum. You're trying to focus attention on the presenter, the person giving the speech or answering the questions and it is a dreadful distraction to have beside and behind him or her numbers of men and women who invariably want to whisper, gesticulate, stare in the wrong direction, scratch their heads, pick their noses or make their exits at completely the wrong moment.

Who is essential is for the organisers to decide, but the 'non-essentials' who sit on platforms are basically either ignorant of the art of presentation or disdainful of it - if they weren't they wouldn't be there.

Generally there are too many bodies on stage and it may be your job to thin them out. I've fought this problem for years at political conferences and gradually we've been able to improve the situation. If you compare the platform parties of the middle and late eighties with those of 1979, the effect is quite noticeable. We've not managed to clear the speaker's part of the platform as entirely as the Americans do, but at least we've managed to create a decent space around the speaker. We set the tone at the Tory Conferences and the other parties have followed suit.

A thirty second commercial on ITV can cost £60,000 or more. If a member of the Government gets ninety seconds of news time, that's worth a lot of money. In that ninety seconds I want every one of the 13 million viewers to concentrate on the speaker - *not* on someone else scratching their nose in the background.

The only exception I would make to this rule is if there are special guests who actually should be 'on-show' because they enhance the programme, for whatever reason. Here, too, you have to be careful and weigh the advantages of their appearance against the disadvantages of their potential to distract from the message.

If you are not in a position to be ruthless about getting rid of people on the platform, school them in the proper way to behave - sitting still, looking towards the speaker and not thumping the table in their enthusiasm. It jolts your carefully prepared and placed microphone out of position and may wobble the lectern as well.

Lectern

Lecterns are a whole subject in themselves but one that frequently gets overlooked.

For a start, a lectern ought to be the right height for each speaker. I know that sounds obvious but even nine years after I designed it, I still have one of the very few adjustable-height lecterns in the UK. More often than not no-one bothers about the height factor, with the result that the speaker may have to peer at his notes or stand awkwardly or otherwise find it impossible to combine proper use of the mike with proper use of the lectern.

The speaker should feel comfortable with the lectern's height and it must be positioned so that he can see his notes. It should be sturdy enough to lean on if necessary. And if you've got more than one speaker it must be adjustable with minimum fuss. We were late in introducing this concept: it took me three years of persuasion for politicians to accept the idea. Billy Graham was using an adjustable lectern twenty-five years ago; (he needed to, since he is six feet four and some of his colleagues are a foot shorter.)

In 1979 I had built a small wind-up lectern for table-top use and followed that a couple of years later with a full-size floor-standing lectern that operates hydraulically. The top half of it slides down over the bottom half so that it can be lowered right down to table-top level when a debate is going on and a speaker is sitting down. At that point he needs to have an uninterrupted view of the audience and they need a clear view of him.

Importantly, the lectern is *never* operated by the speaker who needs full concentration on the speech and presentation. It is operated by a colleague who assesses the right height for each speaker. The levels are marked so that they are visible some feet away; you don't want undignified scrabbling around under a speaker's feet.

This prototype lectern is made of wood with a separate hydraulic unit. It is operated simply by pressing a button. It cost around £2,000 to make in 1982 and the man who built it for me said then that it would 'lift one ton, let alone Willie Whitelaw'.

A lectern should have a minimum depth of 38cm and a minimum width of 50cm - space to hold two A4 sheets alongside each other - and a 'lip' of at least 1.5cm to stop papers sliding off onto the floor.

The lectern at the Guildhall is a classic example of one that looks beautiful but is too small and fragile to use. It's a beautiful creation designed without thought for its function. When Mrs Thatcher speaks at the traditional Lord Mayor's banquet there, we substitute our own humbler but more practical table-top lectern.

Good lecterns today also have space for microphone wiring built into them so that you don't have wire trailing around the place and looking unsightly, or a big boom mike stand in front. (If you are using a table top, cut holes in the baize covering the table to feed the wires through and keep them tidy.)

I like the height of the *lectern* to be adjustable, but the Americans like to adjust the *floor*. This is more expensive but it has a particular advantage in television coverage. It means the cameras can focus on the lectern knowing that the speaker will always be placed in exactly the same position relevant to it. If there are between fifty and two hundred different cameras, as there sometimes are in America, it's a major consideration. In Europe we have to strike a balance between the needs of the audience in the hall and the requirement to communicate effectively to a far larger audience through television.

Autocue

A useful advance in the technology of presentation in the eighties was the advent of the autocue. Ever since I started consultancy work in politics, I'd been pushing for the use of this simple invention - a British one - but it wasn't until after President Reagan used it in his address to the Houses of Parliament that our politicians felt it was worthy of notice.

It is a simple closed circuit television system, a video camera photographing a speech being rolled beneath it. The video monitors are on the floor facing upwards in front of the speaker and there are two pieces of glass above so that the speech is reflected at the speaker's eye-level, directing his main focus at the appropriate part of the audience. In other words, the speaker can read his speech and look out into the audience at the same time. They have a clear view of him and he can hold the important eye contact. The line being spoken is always in the same spot, so that if he turns his head from a familiar sentence he can be confident that he will be able to pick up again where he left off.

When you're reading a speech ordinarily you have either to keep your finger on the spot or find it again. With the autocue, your hands and head are free to communicate body language more powerfully.

The reflector glass can be positioned directly in front of the speaker but I prefer to use wing glasses on either side because it lessens the barrier with the audience and leaves more room for photography. I also surround the monitors discreetly with flowers to avoid distracting the audience.

Use of the autocue is another reason in favour of a variable floor, by the way. When Mrs Thatcher and President Reagan both spoke at the United Nations' 40th Anniversary in 1985 they used the same autocue, which remained in a fixed position. While the President walked off after delivering his speech someone was able to slip in a pre-built ten-centimetre platform for Mrs Thatcher and Rajiv Gandhi, which was a lot less fuss than having to fiddle around re-adjusting the autocue height.

In the UK I commissioned some electrically adjusted autocue screens. Even so, the same rule applies as it does to the lectern: never let the *speaker* adjust the screens to fit his height. Someone else must do it. The autocue operator will be backstage cueing the speed to suit the speaker's delivery. It requires concentration by the operator but, again, I would not let the speaker do it himself.

There is now also a 'computer' autocue - direct projection to the screens by a word processor. It does not have the flexibility of the paper roll and President Reagan, amongst others, always preferred the safety of the mechanical 'roll' with its additional emphasis markings. It is possible to lose the entire speech off a computer disk. You can only lose power with the roll system - and that's much less likely.

It happened however to Ronald Reagan in France once. A power surge blew the fuse on the White House autocue and the President dried-up for a moment and then ad-libbed. I rarely take equipment from one country to another, and never if there is a voltage difference as with the United States (110 volts) and Europe (240 volts). If I need the autocue in America, I have one there and avoid unnecessary problems.

You need to check lighting arrangements with the autocue. If they're wrongly placed they can blank out the screens and make them impossible to read.

Lighting

Lighting is one of the most effective ways of creating a good atmosphere. You can create quite a memorable set out of little more than good lighting. Find out what your venue has to offer and whether you will need to supplement it. Most hotels and similar venues have tracking spotlights and if you have plenty of set-up time, you should be able to cheer up the most basic hotel meeting room.

If television is going to be with you, you will need to arrange stronger lights on the key focal points - you would do well to get a set of four 'redheads' (800 watt TV lights). Incidentally, direct a little light *down* behind the speaker: it fills the space behind him and makes him more three-dimensional.

Find out early on how dark you can make the hall. Dimming the lights is necessary for even the simplest pieces of audio-visual equipment.

Audio-visual equipment

The overhead projector, which shows 11in by 8in (28cm x 20cm) transparencies, can be useful, as can the slide projector. The most consistent mistake with both these pieces of equipment - possibly because they are so simple - is, once again, to have them operated by the speaker. Don't fall into that trap. We've all suffered the 'amateur night' feeling that occurs when the poor speaker gets it wrong: the upside down slide, the image on the ceiling, the missing bulb and the inevitable stifled titters from the audience. The only exception is the small 'teaching' meeting, when the speaker actually draws diagrams on the transparency while talking.

Make sure the equipment is planned, checked and operated by someone who knows what they're doing, and who will *rehearse* with the speakers.

There have been impressive developments of audio-visual aids recently and you might consider some of them if you're staging an ambitious project. Remarkable things can be done linking projectors and computers so that you get composite or varied images on a wall of screens. But there comes a point at which audio-visual presentations take over from being an aid to the speaker and become an end in themselves. If this looks likely, you have to be absolutely certain they're going to achieve your objectives better than a human being!

Generally though, use special effects cautiously and for a specific purpose. It's easy to get carried away by the many tools at your disposal so beware of using them just because they're there.

Once in a while an 'audio extra' creates itself. I was once speaking to some 2,000 people in the Tent Hall in Glasgow when I noticed my audience's attention drifting - something I'm not used to! When I investigated, I found that the long microphone lines across the stage were picking up BBC Radio 2. Since I was behind the public address speakers, I could not hear it. But the audience could. I was being accompanied by an orchestra! Long mike leads need to be properly wired to prevent them from becoming an aerial.

Lasers, helium balloons, streamers, flags, dry ice, disco lights, computer graphics are great at election rallies or festivals but inappropriate at most serious commercial conferences. Sometimes in the art of presentation, 'less is more'.

The backdrop

Take something as simple as a backdrop. It should be interesting but not too interesting, fit in thematically and colour-wise but give a 'clean' backdrop to speakers. It has to be designed or thought out carefully so that conscious decisions can be made about it.

You may decide to put a table and a lectern in front of a blank wall. That's fine as long as you do it deliberately and not by default. At the other extreme you could set up giant screens to show large images of the speaker as we do in larger conferences such as the Institute of Directors at the Royal Albert Hall.

The backdrop should reinforce the message of your conference either overtly - with the slogan or motif emblazoned on it - or subliminally by its design emphasis. If, for instance, your conference is concentrating on leadership and moving into the future, you might design something with a slightly futuristic appearance that left the thought in the minds of the audience without being too obvious about it.

A boon to the organiser who needs a simple mobile improvement for small venues are the 'Supalite' panels, made of coloured foam with metal or plastic edges. They are light, easy to set up and transport and they can cover a multitude of grotty walls.

WINNIN'

When the Royal Sussex hospital called my wife Marlies after the bomb during the 1984 Tory Conference, they told her there had been a 'little accident' but that I was OK.

Marlies thought I had fallen off a ladder fixing a letter G from the conference slogan of that year, 'Britain Winning Through'. The slogan was spelled out in three-foot-high polystyrene lettering and glued onto a soft canvas backdrop. Unfortunately the powerful television lights kept melting the glue, and in spite of extra large dollops of the stuff, the G from 'Winning' fell off every night and I had to be up a ladder fixing it back again at six the next morning. It was too thick to nail and, anyway, the backdrop was too soft.

Now I always glue, nail and use a solid backdrop whenever I can. I think of that episode as my 'belt and braces' lesson.

Sounds right

However your event looks, you still have to be sure that it's going to *sound* good as well. The old adage that a picture is worth a thousand words is small consolation to an audience which can't hear any of them.

If you've got forty or more people, use sound amplification - not necessarily for volume but for *presence*. Like lighting, sound creates atmosphere and lends authority to the proceedings. Some people are daunted by the technology of sound, but it's basically just like water: you can send it out in a jet or you can spray it gently over everyone. Spraying gives the most even coverage and is mostly best for speech. Achieve the

effect by having a number of loudspeakers at lowish level, preferably facing in the same direction. There is no problem with
amplifying a speaker's voice because in a room of any size you
do not hear the individual's voice as such and the electronic
sound reaches everywhere at the same time.

Music is more complicated because electronic sound travels
faster than natural sound, so people hear the 'real' band a
fraction of a second after they've heard its electronic repro-
duction. Music, therefore, should always come from a single
source, not a single loudspeaker but a group of speakers close
enough together for the natural sound to leave the platform at
the same time as the electronic sound. Think of rock concerts
where they have those banks of giant speakers grouped together
on the stage.

Electronic equipment is also built to varying degrees of
power. To continue the water analogy, it's like a fire hose
and a garden hose. You can turn *down* a fire hose to water
a garden, but you cannot turn *up* a garden hose sufficiently
to tackle a fire. Powerful amplifiers can be turned down for a
small hall, but a weak amplifier has no potential for increased
volume before it starts distorting the sound. To get good quality
sound in a meeting, therefore, have fifty per cent more power
than the sound man says you need.

A rough guide, until you work out your own preferences, is
to look for amplifiers of 100 watts for meetings up to 150 people;
200 watts up to 500 people; 500 watts up to 1,000 people and
1,000-1,500 watts up to 3,000 people. For larger groups you
will need supplementary power and sound sources.

The acoustics (the factor that determines how sound behaves)
are different at every venue. Outdoors, sound will 'evaporate',
so you need to compensate with more power. With good acoustics a hall will distribute sound evenly. People soak up sound.
You need more volume for a full hall than an empty one, so
allow for that when you're testing - which will probably be in
an empty hall.

Watch out for metal roofs and high ceilings: they'll make
the sound bounce around like water off a tin roof. The Royal
Albert Hall has acoustic panels in the roof to absorb bouncing

sound. In Earls Court in 1966, before the days of good acoustic panels, we draped silk parachutes from the roof in an attempt to cut down the echo; nowadays technology helps!

There was a strange side effect to the cleaning of the Winter Gardens Empress Ballroom in Blackpool, which was cleaned and restored to its original Victorian splendour in 1984. The ballroom *looked* beautiful but when Sir Basil Feldman stood up to give the opening address at the Conservative Conference, though his projection was fine and his microphone working, half his audience had difficulty hearing, and a third were hearing twice. You see, when they took a century's dust and dirt off those walls, they completely changed the acoustics, swapping grubby absorbency for beautiful, bright marble which bounced the sound all over the place.

Beware of feedback, the dreadful shriek or whistle when a microphone is in front of a loudspeaker (the inanimate, not the human kind). What happens is that the mike hears the sound going into it, being amplified by the system and then coming out louder behind it again. This noise then 'feeds back' into the microphone again, causing that awful sound and complete confusion.

If you get a little 'ringing' in the microphone sound, try a little less 'treble' on the tone controls. You can change the tone of treble or base. A balace is possible for both music and speech and the right adjustment will make a noticeable difference.

Each individual sound source, microphone, tape recorder etc, will have its own level control into the amplifier or mixer. When you are testing, balance the volumes of the different sources. You will then find a master volume control on the amplifier that raises the whole (balanced) mix to the right level for that audience without affecting the balance of the individual sources.

Test your mikes for sensitivity, tone, pick-up range, best position and so on before the proper 'balance' check. Play with them without an audience, but remember to make adjustments when the audience is present.

Ability with sound systems only comes with practice and the more you learn about sound, the more respect you have for it. It is seldom simple and even the more experienced operators make mistakes, often because they do not understand the difference between *source* - what the original sound is like - and *acoustics* - what happens to it when it leaves the loudspeakers.

At Billy Graham's 1961 Maine Road Stadium Crusade, low-level, multi-speaker systems meant that music from choir and instruments was travelling around the stadium electronically and then being 'chased' by the real sound, with the result that everyone heard everything at least twice. We had to build sound 'towers' by the stage to get the music amplification right.

With Billy Graham again at the Lausanne Olympic Stadium in 1974, we had made no allowance for the effect of the wind on sound - it blows it around like rain. Some of the time the Germans at one end of the stadium were hearing the French translation, while their own language was floating with the wind over the top of the stadium and down to Lake Geneva.

QUESTION OF INTERPRETATION

In the Euro 70 television crusade from Dortmund in Germany, we reached thirty-six cities in twelve countries through live closed circuit television on big screens: 100,000 people a night watched around Europe.

The speech was translated phrase by phrase into six languages. Billy Graham would say, 'Good evening, ladies and gentlemen' and six translators would repeat the phrase in their own languages, their mikes feeding the appropriate centres. Each pair of interpreters was in a small booth by the Dortmund platform with one microphone, a cut-off button and a television showing the broadcast picture.

There was discussion after the first night between the Welsh interpreters, Rheinallt Williams and David Sheppard. Wouldn't it be better not to translate Billy's invitation to come forward, as the people at the Welsh meeting understood English and it allowed a quiet moment between Billy's phrases?

'Well, last night,' said Rheinallt, 'I kept right on interpreting Billy through the invitation.'

'Oh no you didn't, Rheinallt,' said David. 'I had my finger on the button.'

Rehearse

Rehearsal pays - and steers you around disasters. That means rehearsing *everything*. If necessary climb the scaffolding yourself to get the lights right. Don't take it for granted that they'll be OK. Try out the PA system on site; don't take the management's word that they'll do it for you. You'll arrive to find they've stuck the mikes just where you don't want them.

Work out and run through your lighting and music cues. Music that is to be played as part of a programme must be chosen with care. 'Don't Cry For Me Argentina' isn't quite right for a Falklands Veterans' meeting. I have some fun sometimes though. We played 'Who Wants To Be A Millionaire' during the collection at one big conference.

National Anthems - never assume your venue will have one on tape. At one meeting a chairman blithely told me as he went on to the platform that they *would* have the National Anthem at the end, changing his mind without consulting me first. I didn't have a recording of it with me, Mrs Thatcher was already on her feet and there was no way I could interrupt to reverse the decision.

I managed to get a police car to rush me through security to the shopping precinct. I dashed into a record shop, begged a loan of the album, transferred it onto cassette in Dixon's next door, sped back to the hall and managed to shove it into the system just as the chairman announced it and the audience was standing. I now carry one with me everywhere. But if you're thinking of doing the same, make sure you get a recording that can be sung-along with and not one of those dragged out funereal dirge versions.

Everything needs rehearsal and not just in the venue. If you are on a site-recce and you hit on an idea or a way of solving your problem, do a dry run. Someone will say they've got a machine that prints names on badges. The machine can completely fail to work because no-one has bothered to test it before the day.

In 1988, I was producing a major women's conference at the Barbican and we needed a big bank of flowers. Twenty-odd years earlier, I'd picked up an idea from the marvellously crea-tive Bill Brown who was Director of Billy Graham's Crusades in 1966–67. I was his assistant and when he wanted flowers he would send me to the old Covent Garden at 4.30am to buy hundreds of pots of chrysanthemums which would then be sold off at the end of the day, thus serving a dual purpose as decoration and a means of recouping some of our costs.

I realised things might not be the same nowadays so, ten days before the conference, my assistant Joanne and I went down to Covent Garden (which is now at Nine Elms) and had a trial run. We discoverd that you now need £2 to get in *and* give a week's notice for 300 pots. If we'd left it to the day we'd have been sunk!

Co-ordination

One person has to be responsible for co-ordinating all these different elements and the need for an integrated approach, with one person carrying the overview, was brought home sharply to me during a Youth Conference in Eastbourne in 1983. My wife and I were actually in Hawaii at the time (combining busi-ness and pleasure) secure, or so I thought, in the knowledge that everything was running smoothly.

In fact just about everything that could go wrong went wrong. The television lighting shone right into the autocue, dazzling the speakers and making the apparatus unusable. Staff got frazzled, speakers got angry and there was almost a fist fight between some of my colleagues and the lighting technicians. Someone had brought the adjustable lectern and set it up perfectly but not bothered to find out the heights of the speakers. And so it went on. The problem was not that people had not done their jobs: they had. But they had only done their *own* jobs. What was lacking was the professional overview.

The resulting chaos was so memorable that I've never dared take a holiday during a conference again!

Get there early

If you have the co-ordinating role, an important priority is to be everywhere early. If a conference is due to start at 9.30am, be there at 6.30am. That way you have time to find problems - and put them right. You have time to digest the unexpected worm, as they say about early birds!

Most 'organisers' swan in at eight-thirty looking important, only to discover there's a big hitch and they have no time to put it right. And the craziest things can happen at the last minute.

There was a youth dance during one conference I staged and at six the next morning I did an automatic check on the adjustable lectern, only to find graffiti-covered papers stuck all over the front. They didn't show when the lectern was down, but imagine the audience's laughter if they had popped up with the lectern and the speaker. It took us one and a half hours to clean up, but my early start gave us plenty of time.

No audience wants to start off with blunders. You have a long way to go to win them back.

In Southport recently we had planned a 30ft (9m) Portakabin to serve as part of a wall around a car park. Someone somewhere, however, changed the order for the Portakabin and we ended up with a 15ft (4.5m) one. We then didn't have enough materials for the wall so we had to shorten its length, which in turn meant there was not enough room for media vehicles and not enough space for VIPs to manoeuvre their cars in, and that meant altering security arrangements. All these complications arose simply because someone thought a smaller cabin would be big enough but had not bothered to consult the professionals.

Once in Porthcawl in South Wales I was trying out my hydraulic lectern and discovered it had developed a horrible squeak. Again I had *time* to find a garage that had opened early and had a welder. We got him to come and fix it before the first session.

At a Local Government conference, someone at the venue had put up the mikes but had not checked to make sure they were fixed properly, so they were slowly drooping! Mikes always need careful adjusting to catch the speaker's voice - but not, hopefully, his eye!

At yet another conference, police dogs searching the hall before the opening session broke the teleprompter!

Your excessively early arrival means that you can check the aforesaid dogs are not using your beautiful flower arrangements as their loo, and also run through a technical check and the autocue before anyone else gets there. (That's how you discover the odd rude word that's been written on the script by some joker, before the VIP inadvertently reads it out.)

Be nice to staff and volunteers, as much as possible! One well-known television personality is said to be rather hard on the teleprompter operators. At a live broadcast he started to read his autocue lines - 'Hello and good evening. You're on your own now - we've gone home!'

COST FACTOR

Staging needs an imaginative mind! And occasionally you have to balance results and cost.

A director filming on location in a stadium was spending £20,000 per hour. His assistant should have directed a scene after lunch but the director returned to find things at a standstill. 'Why no filming?' he asked. 'We can't find the caretaker to open the locker-room door,' replied the assistant.

'Kick the thing down,' said the director. 'The delay has cost £20,000 and we can buy a gold door to replace it for less than that.'

Part Three
CAMPAIGN TRAIL

8
PROJECTING THE IMAGE

A man, Sir, should keep his friendship
in constant repair.

Samuel Johnson

The most exciting and terrifying thing about political campaigning is that it is a tangible measure of your communication skills. In the other fields I've discussed earlier - public speaking, appearing on television, staging a special event, holding a conference, you can (but you shouldn't) kid yourself that they went better than they really did. But in an election the facts speak for themselves; if you do not get the right message across to the right people, you lose. This applies whether you are trying to get yourself elected as a parent governor, a church committee member, or a party leader.

Now, let's get something clear at the beginning. As with any other effort to make an impact, if you want to be successful you must have *substance* in your message. A quality product - fillet steak not offal! But, once you have the steak, it is the sizzle, the tantalising, mouth-watering aroma, the surrounding cleanliness and the personal credibility of the butcher and the chef that persuades the customer to choose it.

Political campaigning goes on all the time of course, not just in the run-up to a major election. That is just the intensification, the high point of an ongoing process. In the UK the political parties maintain a permanent grass roots organisation for this reason.

In America the organisational style is geared to mobilise people only for specific projects. By instinct, the Americans are geared to winning, the British to playing the game. The Americans recognise that professionals can achieve more; the British resent the professionals interfering in what is 'always done'.

Fortunately, in the eighties we have begun to recognise

that modern communication skills go far beyond the concept of advertising. Even so, when we gathered together a superb voluntary team of some of the UK's top communicators for both the 1983 and 1987 General Elections, the Conservative Party could not find any strategic use for them. The groups contained some of the most talented, creative, experienced and successful people in UK marketing and public relations. In effect the equivalent of a million pounds-worth of fees went unused.

The Americans have learned to bring in their big guns whenever they need them. The Republicans and Democrats tick over with a skeleton staff and then hire specialist consultants for each campaign. The directors of the 1988 Republican National Convention, for example, were political campaign experts seconded from their companies in Washington to the New Orleans event for six months.

In theory, our system *ought* to work better. If we had a well-oiled party machine, we should be able to move into a higher gear every now and again to win elections. In practice it doesn't. It makes people stale and dull.

We need a radical reassessment of what our *organisational goals* are and how we will achieve them. Getting your supporters enthusiastic at the right time requires strategy and planning and that is a political weakness in the UK.

I've been advised to stay away from political jokes (they too often get elected) but in the UK, party workers say: 'If you put a monkey up for Parliament here and stuck a red (or blue) rosette on him, he'd get in.' The point they are making is that, for the most part, people still vote more for political parties in Britain than for the individual candidate.

In America it's the opposite, especially in presidential elections. There, voters opt for the individual and a big chunk of campaign money is spent on what we call 'name identification' - getting voters to know *your* candidate's name.

Political agents in the UK often refer to their candidates as 'an unfortunate necessity'. He (or she) could get in the way of the running of the party machine. But, thank goodness, that is changing. The human side of politics is getting stronger.

It's never been clear though, if you have a Conservative seat, say, in the West Midlands, whether people vote because they think Mrs Thatcher is doing a good job, or because they are worried about a local problem, or because Mrs McJones next door was helped by the sitting candidate over her rates problem!

People are influenced not just by political parties or candidates but also by national, regional and local considerations. In some seats there will be a substantial personal vote for a long-serving, well-liked MP. When such MPs die or step down the resulting by-election often provides big shock waves.

Crosby in 1981 was a classic example: the voters lost a man they had known for thirty years and they didn't know who to vote for instead. There was virtually no constituency organisation to cope with a major campaign - it had not been needed for three decades! Shirley Williams stumbled on to the scene and a 19,000 Conservative majority turned into a 5,000 SDP (1981 version) one.

By the time the General Election arrived eighteen months later, there was a good candidate (Malcolm Thornton, now MP), a renewed constituency organisation and time for the people of Crosby to realise what they'd done in that panicky moment when they were looking for a familiar face as their Member of Parliament.

Some trends happen without anyone being quite sure why. For instance, if a party does well in local government elections in May, it is likely to do well in another election a month later despite the fact that the local authority is quite separate from the Westminster or European Parliaments. But it would be a mistake to conclude that the results *must* be similar. Separate strategic planning and professional campaigning could produce substantially different results in two such campaigns.

Voting patterns are a complex business and my colleague, Keith Britto, who is an expert in these things, tells me that no research has been able to disentangle all the strands of voting motivation, a crucial point to remember in planning a campaign!

Atmosphere and environment: national and local

There are two elements in an election at every level from parish council to national government - environment and organisation.

By environment I mean the mood, the atmosphere of the campaign, its tone and the preoccupations of the voters. These determine the priorities of the campaign and the emphasis on projecting the image of the party and its people. The organisation, local and national, has to build on this environment and use it as powerfully as possible.

National activity highlights the parties, the leaders and most of the issues. If the national mood is wrong, even the very best organisation is unlikely to win a local election.

The local emphasis more often needs to be on the candidate, getting his name, face, personality and position known in the community and introducing him to key groups of people. As I said earlier, name identification campaigns are routine in the United States but not so common in Europe, although there have been cases where a candidate has been so successfully promoted that he has won, despite his local party's unpopularity at the time.

As a military analogy, with the (political) campaign as your battleground, the generals at headquarters would gather intelligence, study the enemy, develop overall strategy, and provide hardware and ammunition. It is the troops on the ground who do most of the fighting. The troops must be enthusiastic, well briefed, well equipped - *and* in touch with headquarters!

It's always said that Oppositions rarely win elections, Governments lose them. It was Jim Callaghan's dithering in 1978 and failure to anticipate the horrors and effect of the 'winter of discontent' that contributed substantially to Labour's defeat in the General Election the following year. By then they were running round frantically trying to excuse everything that had happened. They broke the basic rule of presentation which applies in politics as much as it does in other fields. Whatever you do, do it deliberately: be seen to be in control of the situation. Just saying, 'Crisis, what crisis? is *not* the way to do it.

In 1979 Labour was obviously in a panic - that set the mood. The Tory party used that atmosphere to its advantage and combined it with its organisational skills to produce a Conservative victory.

Just the facts, m'am - just the facts!

Before you start thinking about mood and atmosphere, or revving up the party machine, what you *must* have are the facts. What are the voters in your electoral area thinking and feeling?

The foundation of all political campaigning has to be opinion research. In national terms this must be done professionally. Locally it needs to be done to as near a professional standard as possible. What will *not* do - though you'd be surprised how often this happens anyway - is a group of political activists getting together and saying, 'Auntie Flo thinks that . . .' or 'I think a good slogan would be : . .'

You need qualitative and quantitative research. First, a small representative group discussing subjects in depth with a trained observer leading and reporting conclusions. Then quantitative research, testing those themes, reactions and conclusions on a larger sample of people. If your research is good, it gives you the base from which to start. You take the nasty results with the nice, examine them thoroughly and dispassionately and ask these questions:

What are people really concerned about?
What do they think of us and our opponents at this moment?
What would change their thinking?
What do they want from us?

Before you take off on your campaign, be sure you know whether you can genuinely meet the voters' needs, without compromising your convictions and standards. When you can, your campaigning will reflect it. When you can't, you have to explain why you can't and try to convert the voters. Just proving that you are right and they are wrong will lose the election for you. You *must* win the hearts as well as the minds.

The fact that you're dealing with abstracts makes it hard. If voters say they want politicians to care, how do you show it - you can't suddenly burst into tears. The Conservatives have always had to tackle this particular problem by tying care in with action and results. Not only did we care, we did something about it. Not only did we *want* to improve something but we have created the wealth to make more resources and improvements available for social needs.

What you say during a political campaign is the concrete foundation of it. It is however at most only ten per cent of the *impact* of the communication. The rest is presentation.

THE 'X' FACTOR

Here are two examples of involuntary agenda emphasis, the situation where the agenda is set by events beyond the control of politicians.

In the 1988 General Election in Sweden the Social Democrats had a huge sympathy vote lingering on after the murder of Olaf Palme while he had been Prime Minister some years before. So despite a good campaign by the Moderate Party and some dissatisfaction with the Social Democrats, the emotional factor still returned the Social Democrats to power.

In Denmark the same year Prime Minister Schluter went to the polls after a social democrat coalition defeated him in Parliament and ruled that NATO ships coming to Denmark must be nuclear weapon free. It was doubtful whether Schluter could remain in control but two emotional anniversaries during the campaign helped to keep defence as *the* issue: April 9 was the anniversary of the German invasion and occupation of Denmark in the Second World War, and May 9 the anniversary of the Liberation. Schluter won.

The image

An 'image' is projected not created. If you do not have the substance you will fail, even with the help of 'media coaches' and 'image creators'. If they were that good they would have told you to forget it until you had a good message or product to project!

As that great veteran of many political campaigns, Lord Thorneycroft, said in 1978: 'In the end, Harvey, image is what you are.' You cannot project a phoney. That is why Labour's campaign failed in 1987. Glitz, glamour and gloss cannot replace substance, they can only enhance it.

The word 'image' conjures up something insubstantial, an illusion, a gimmick. In fact it's just the opposite. When you project an image, you project an intensified version of the original. A clarified version of a reality. The man or woman in the street cannot know their leaders personally. But they can 'know' them, in the sense of getting a feel for the sort of person they are, a closeness with them, even an affection.

That's what image means and it's what we try to do in political campaigns. We project the politicians beyond their immediate circle of personal contacts out to the people who matter. *What* we project is the essence of our politicians, the nature of their convictions. It's making the most of what you've got.

Projecting the image

The first and most powerful image projector today is television. Everybody has access to it and politicians ignore it only if they are thick or arrogant.

It is tempting to fantasise that leaders and parties make their reputations through finely tuned arguments in the House of Commons or speeches in far-flung halls. The truth is that political leaders project their image nowadays in ninety-second 'sound bites' on radio and television.

Advertising is a one-way hard-sell in a political campaign and can be a good motivator as long as it doesn't try to sell the voter something his guts tell him isn't true. It can also help to set the debate agenda if it is strategically planned. It is, however, a reinforcer and emphasiser, not a converter.

A girl sits down with a man and he says, 'I'm very romantic' - that's advertising.

A girl sits down with a man and he says, 'What you need is a good romance and it so happens I'm very romantic' - that's marketing.

A girl sits down with a man and *she* says, 'I hear you're very romantic, please take me to dinner' - that's Public Relations!

Newspapers do develop the discussion in much more detail, but people are more likely to be turned off by newspapers than on, so their effect is negative rather than positive. The written press provides back-up, analysis and in-depth knowledge but rarely encourages or inspires people. That comes from television.

To put it another way: people get their minds going from newspapers and their hearts moving from TV. And we win the heart first, *then* the mind.

How individuals come across on television usually depends on how much understanding, effort and practice they are prepared to give to it. I've discussed this in the chapter on radio and television. In a political campaign, television exposure is magnified many times, so the projection of the image has to be co-ordinated, consistent and continuous. Though you project, not create, an image, with a proper understanding of broadcasting you can create opportunities for politicians to project themselves.

If the public is to get the message, it must be presented to them many times. We therefore combine television and newspaper coverage. The viewers get a glimpse of an event or person on the early evening news, another taste at nine or ten in the evening and (hopefully) a bit more detail and not too much distraction in the following morning's papers, radio and TV.

Media images

I sat in a thirteenth-century hall in Bruges in September 1988 and listened to Mrs Thatcher's speech on the future of Europe. It was one of the most powerful, positive and visionary speeches I have heard her give in eleven years. I got up feeling encouraged and thoroughly supporting her strong positive vision of Europe's future.

The next morning the newspapers headlined what I thought was a completely different 'anti-Europe' speech. I even wondered just for a moment if she had, unknown to me, made another, negative, speech later in the day. It was only weeks after the speech that I began to read in the press that actually her theme had been positive and she had presented a positive forward view.

The media had 'created' a false 'image' of an anti-Europe Mrs Thatcher, but because it *was* 'created', without substance, from a small out-of-context part of her argument, it didn't last long.

In 1980 I was at the Cleveland debate between Ronald Reagan and Jimmy Carter. On television and in person, it was vividly clear that Reagan won at least 9 to 1. In the Bush-Dukakis debate in 1988, Bush won at least 7 to 3.

On both occasions the press reported a draw or a very close thing because they were concerned only with the mind, the argument. Television projected to the *hearts* of the people and we know the results.

The Telly

Some people purport to be experts in political campaigning but still refuse to accept television as a major medium. They think that gearing a campaign towards maximum effective coverage is demeaning. They are either blind or foolish. After personal contact, television is the fastest and most powerful way of winning people. We who have been classed as 'image-makers' in Europe and the United States are proud of the job we do.

I have worked with and studied strategical political cam-
I have worked with and studied strategical political

campaigning in many countries, among them France, Germany, Malta, Norway, the United Kingdom and the United States. In every case television in its full variety of formats has been the primary influence in projecting the parties' images.

In Malta in 1981 we faced a socialist black-out of the Centre Nationalist Party from any access to Maltese television. The Nationalists set up their own TV station in Sicily and beamed into Malta. An estimated fifty per cent of the Maltese population watched those broadcasts and the Nationalists won 50.7 per cent of the votes.

Elections can be and are won or lost on television. An image can change on that screen suddenly and dramatically. When George Bush addressed the Republican National Convention in New Orleans in 1988, he was still seen as a wimp. He was still behind in the polls. His fortune changed suddenly and dramatically when all America watched his acceptance speech on TV.

I had got myself down on the floor of the Superdome Convention Hall to make a video. He began his speech in fairly predictable, George Bush style, slow and a bit boring. Then he said dryly: 'We're not going to be too hard on our Democrat opponents. I'm going to work at keeping my charisma in check.'

Suddenly, I felt the atmosphere change. People were no longer thinking, 'He's all we've got - we'll probably be OK', instead it was 'This guy is big enough to laugh at himself. He's going to be President, and a good one.' It sunk into 30,000 delegates and millions watching at home that this man *knew* he was not a charismatic orator but he *knew*, too, that he was going to be President and he could handle it.

He showed us George Bush, the man, as well as the politician. It goes back to my point that genuineness is the key. If you've got it, flaut it.

In his thirty-first year in show business, Cliff Richard was the top of the UK pops for Christmas 1988. His No 1 was 'Mistletoe and Wine' - a song of his Christian testimony. The pop world expected 'Silent Night' by the group Bros to oust Cliff. With exaggerated hype, 'Silent Night' climbed to second place, but at Christmas it was Cliff No 1 and Bros behind him. Two Christmas songs. The difference? Cliff's conviction showed.

People respond to gut genuineness in a way that they cannot respond to phoney image.

The televised debate in October 1988 between Bush and Dukakis was virtually a repeat, in terms of people-winning, of Reagan/Carter in 1980. Television showed Reagan and Carter as they were. Reagan genuine, confident, warm and human. Carter cold, stiff, impersonal and lacking confidence. People liked what they saw in Reagan and the campaign was won in that debate.

Dukakis had similar flaws to Carter: lack of political substance and lack of belief in what he himself had to say. He said 'I think I'm fairly lovable' - with a face as cold and unlovable as if he were dissecting a fish rather than trying to reach his fellow human beings.

Later in the campaign his media advisers tried desperately to 'create' a new Dukakis by injecting comments such as 'I am a liberal, I am against capital punishment but I would feel like killing the person who harmed my wife and children.'

Of course it didn't work! Bush's belief in what he was saying was obvious. Dukakis seemed to be reciting words merely to try to manipulate voters. If your body language, eyes, mouth, expression and voice contradict the words you are saying, the words will be meaningless and even counter-productive. If you have nothing to say, don't open your mouth and prove it.

Dukakis's television performance and interviews gave it all away, as did those of his supporters. They *knew* they were going to lose. The newspapers in Europe were seriously claiming the battle was close and that Dukakis could even win enough States to pull it off. But *he* knew he couldn't and his supporters knew it. They used phrases like 'We're going to surprise them', 'It's going to be real competitive.' They were going through the motions on television but their voices, face and body language were vividly clear - they knew they would lose and they were putting on a brave front.

What they may *not* have realised is that that message conveyed itself to the American public! Television is the most personal and intimate communication medium there is. When you're on it make sure you believe what you're saying!

DEBATING POINT

Good presentation points to and highlights the message at the heart.

When Jimmy Carter suggested that the world would be a dangerous place if Ronald Reagan became President (at their televised debate in Cleveland in 1980), Reagan replied: 'There you go again, Jimmy,' and smilingly put Carter right on some facts.

What that sentence *really* said to the audience and viewers was: 'It's people who matter to me and I'm going to take care of my fellow Americans real well.'

When Carter a few minutes later in the debate said, 'I asked my [eight-year-old] daughter Amy last night what she thought . . .', what the audience *heard* was: 'I'd better try to find a warm human illustration before it's too late.'

He was too late!

Co-ordination

Projecting an image, particularly in Europe, is not just maximising the television potential of particular people. It is also about carrying that image into every other aspect of the political campaign, so that the whole really is greater than the sum of the parts. The image has to be both of the politician and of the party. Professionally the two *should* go together. A local candidate at variance with the national campaign may please the press but it rarely wins the people.

In developing an image, you and your workers, professional or voluntary, have to swallow your pride, smile at yourselves and put yourselves in second place to getting the message across - not easy, not often said, but true! So face it.

All too often in politics we are handicapped by the fact that Mrs Jones has done something a certain way for twenty-seven years and therefore must be allowed to do it again this time. The real world has long left behind the age when old so-and-so could decide 'I rather like this slogan' or 'My constituents think we ought to do such and such' without that 'feeling' being backed up by professional research and experience.

In the Church and in politics we are cursed by a number of opposite extremes. 'If it was good enough for the Apostle Paul/Disraeli it's good enough for me' at one end. Or, 'We've got to be high-tech, use computers' at the other. 'All this American razzamatazz, we don't want it here' - or, 'Let's have balloons and bands for everything.'

It's not 'playing the game' that is most important; it's winning, and a professional assessment of which methods will achieve that. And just in case it is suggested that I'm saying the end justifies the means, let me confirm that I'm not. You can assume that I mean legitimate, ethical and otherwise proper methods.

Now I would not ignore hunches, insight or occasional flashes of brilliance that can come from anybody, as long as they do not become a substitute for objectivity and professionalism. Today's political campaigning requires trained and experienced communicators familiar with modern practices in opinion research, public relations and marketing. That means understanding the principles of communication and custom-applying them to a campaign, not just throwing hardware at people and showing them the switches. So if you are serious about winning, put your prejudices away and start again. (People often believe they are thinking when they are merely rearranging their prejudices.)

Technology is not just about making clever films for party political broadcasts or staging breathtaking rallies, but more about helping weld your communications strategy into a coherent whole.

For years we have had the technology for every constituency headquarters to be linked to a central databank of key information. Every candidate can have *instant* access to the national leaders' comments. The candidate can call up the data and be briefed throughout the day about new statistics, party policy developments and relevant events. Sadly, because our party political management systems have had to centre on 'now', these strategic concepts are slow in coming into use.

Such technology, properly used, would more than pay its way, coming into its own during the intensity of an election but maintaining its worth all year round in enabling swift and efficient communication between headquarters and members. I'm not referring to top secret information; if the other parties are interested enough to hack their way into the system, they might be converted!

While I'm on the subject of secrecy, it is true to say that many politicians, sometimes justifiably, are paranoid about the subject. Fair enough at senior government level when there are so many 'leaks' in the system. Nonetheless, it is impossible to carry out a strategy if those who are meant to implement it don't know what it is!

The image you are projecting for your campaign will not be confined to people. It must be echoed in slogans, posters, the visual design of venues for meetings, speeches, interviews, rallies and press releases. There must be a unity of concept and content in everything from your banners to the banner headlines. It is known commercially as a 'corporate identity'.

An image, after all, is the way people *see* you. If you are not prepared to project it properly, it is most likely that people will only see the wrong parts!

A campaign strategy needs to have an in-built system of self-criticism and self-assessment. How are the plans being carried out? How effective are they being in achieving your objective? What can be done to make them more successful? You need flexibility to change tack if you are not getting it right.

Be aware of the time limit: no election campaign goes on for more than three or four weeks in the United Kingdom - be glad about that! People have a limited capacity to sustain interest in politics. It's one reason why there is so much apathy in America where campaigns seem never-ending.

Don't let time overtake you. This was a major mistake in the Dukakis camp. The Democrats clearly felt guilty about their 'liberal' politics and thus uneasy when Bush attacked them. Their initial response was denial. Then, far too late anyway, the Dukakis advisors decided to change tack and try to make 'liberalism' sound decent by linking it to names from the past like Kennedy and Truman.

It was so obviously a panic reaction that it fooled nobody. Not only had they failed to think it through under the 'what if' strategic planning heading, but they had also failed to consider how they were going to project the change or how the people were going to react. They had made the more usually British mistake of asking 'What shall we do?' rather than the standard American approach of 'What has to be done to achieve our objectives?'

On the whole, especially at local level, the Left in Britain has been more goal orientated than the Right. When the Left want to take control of a particular constituency, they look at its controlling group and note that over a six-month period the maximum number of people attending the decision-making meetings is never more than (say) twenty-seven.

Question: 'What is our aim?' Answer: 'Control.'

Question: 'How do we get it?' Answer: 'Get fourteen people to vote for us.'

Then they select fourteen people and go after them one by one.

It is no good complaining about militants running everything if we have not spotted what is happening because we're so busy doing it the way 'we always do'.

In America, campaign leaders ask: 'How much money do we need to do the job properly?' They then look at that figure, break it down into separate realistic amounts achievable in various ways and set up the systems that are going to raise that cash.

In the UK we say: 'How much money have we got? Oh dear, we'll have to run the project on that budget.'

A winning strategy

A winning campaign strategy comes from answers to the questions: What must we do to get our supporters to turn out on the day? What must we do to firm up the opinion of those who almost support us? How many people do we need to convert?

And what must we do to neutralise the opposition?

I believe that campaigns should be at least 70 per cent positive for your side and no more than 30 per cent knocking your opponents. Ideally I like to see a ratio of 85 per cent positive, 15 per cent negative. I don't like heavy knocking campaigns which at best seem sour and at worst backfire. In Opposition, of course, you have to criticise harder but that criticism has to be *seen* to be reasonable if you are to succeed.

Dukakis on defence and crime and Kinnock on defence and the economy were *perceived* to be weak. They failed to pick their own high ground or to control the political agenda.

We cannot lose touch with political reality. What do we do, for example, about the Opposition? Do we knock them, ignore them or try to discourage their supporters from voting?

There are elections at all levels where it can be better for a party to have a low turn-out overall because those who do vote will tend to be your people. Everyone is *free* to vote, but your objective is to win - not to guarantee a high turn-out! If you run a high-profile, fancy campaign it will alert everyone to the fact that they should be voting and the proportion in your favour could shrink rapidly. It may be better to run a low key affair targeted directly at your own supporters.

Perhaps I should point out here that there's a distinction between the before and the after of an election. Once someone is elected they serve *every* member of that constituency, antis as well as pros. While campaigning you owe it to your convictions to do the best you can to *win*.

I've watched a lot of American campaigning at close quarters including the primaries and presidential election of 1980, the Republican Convention in 1984 (when I also spent a week travelling with Ronald Reagan) and the most recent Republican Convention in New Orleans in 1988. There is a lot we can learn from them without having to copy slavishly.

The Conservative Party in this country has been hindered by the concept that winning the argument automatically means winning the people. The Socialists have historically been better at going for the gut-level reaction.

It's only really in the last two general elections that we

have begun to bring fun and excitement into campaigns, to raise people's enthusiasm to the point where they can let down their reserve a little bit. The other parties have followed the Conservative lead and we have completely changed the face of political presentation since the early 1980s.

We're no less serious of purpose today but we may now seem a little less po-faced. In that way the electorate see us as people first, Conservatives second and politicians third. And that's the way it should be!

STRANGE SEAT MATES

On one of my planning visits to Washington I sat next to a pleasant young lady on the plane out. We chatted a little after the movie and well out over the Atlantic at 37,000ft I commented that a lot of my consultancy work was with the British Conservative Party. 'What funny seat mates,' she said, 'I'm with the IRA.'

And she was. I checked her out with the FBI and she raised funds for the IRA in the United States - not illegal at that time - and carried the money across to her IRA contacts every month. I told her that I had been involved in one of the IRA attacks when I had been blown up in the Brighton Bomb, and that I had friends and colleagues who had been badly hurt or killed.

'I have nothing against you personally,' she told me quietly, 'but that was one of the happiest days in my life - we almost brought the Thatcher Government down.'

Sad - she was bright, educated and charming; but with such a bitter heart. In the end, image is what you are!

9
NURTURING THE GRASS ROOTS

The humblest citizen of all the land,
when clad in the armour of a righteous cause,
is stronger than all the hosts of Error.
William Jennings Bryan

People power

Technology is a wonderful thing and I'm one of its greatest fans. I use it throughout my work because, used skilfully and imaginatively, it can make any sort of communication more powerful, more exciting and frequently a lot more fun.

But if you want your message to have impact you need people-power first and foremost. This is especially true in political campaigning. You can have first-rate candidates, experienced political and communications professionals and all the sophisticated equipment money can buy, but if you don't have the grass roots organisation as back up you will probably fail.

The professionals motivate, guide, provide resources and strategy, but at the heart of a political campaign are its voluntary workers. No politician or party can function without such an army. They decide whether you win or lose. If you have a strong enough army of voluntary workers you can conquer the world, or even turn the People's Republic of Islington blue!

America and Germany are countries which are particularly good at recruiting and keeping in regular contact with their supporters, which makes it far easier to galvanise them when you need them most in the run-up to an election. We for the most part are bad at this. We approach it in a hit-and-miss sort of way instead of through a systematic communication programme.

Direct Mail

One of the most effective ways to recruit and encourage members and supporters is by direct mail. You can target particular groups you think are likely supporters, draw a response and then keep in touch.

The Christian Democrats in Germany have a tradition of good quality newspapers. They are well-produced, have interesting human and political content and are mailed (not hopefully dumped in offices for volunteers to deliver) to 600,000 party members every month. Members are kept in touch with party people and activities, political news and views and social events. They stay interested and involved.

The Americans specialise in the personal touch with individualised laser-printed letters. They are also skilful in their deployment of famous names. It's a rare person who can ignore a letter sent personally to him over the signature of Clint Eastwood or Charlton Heston, saying 'I need your help'.

I've been involved in direct mail ever since my first days with the Billy Graham Organisation in the early sixties. We pioneered the technique well before it became used on so large a scale by giants like American Express and Reader's Digest. As with any technique, direct mail has basic principles which must be obeyed if the programme is to communicate and raise money over a long period:

* It must be regular (a minimum of eight times a year)
* It must be personal, relevant and informal
* It must be good quality
* It must *ask for* and *offer* something
* It must appeal to emotion first and reason second

As we enter the nineties we are progressing slowly with direct mail in UK politics, but national attempts by the different parties have failed for one reason or another. Mostly they're haphazard so that you don't hear anything for months at a stretch, or they're impersonal, or the responses are not followed-up and developed, or they are stupefyingly dull. That's probably the worst sin. Who wants to be involved with a boring organisation?

There are regulations governing how much can be spent during election campaigns. These vary from country to country and obviously you have to be aware of them and comply with them. Outside the campaign itself, however, you can spend whatever you can raise. Money is well spent in setting up and maintaining a properly serviced grass roots party organisation. A good direct mail programme will hold them together and bring their response. Everyone likes to feel wanted and appreciated and such a group of people will give or raise whatever amount of money is needed. We raised £2 million in eighteen months for Luis Palau's Mission to London in 1984, most of it through direct mail.

In 1979 we began pioneering the direct mail concept at constituency level with my wife Marlies at first typing and then working the word processor and computer. A constituency operation in south-east London was begun at about the same time. The prevailing idea then among Conservatives was that computers were 'hi-falutin' and 'impersonal'. I never could understand why a letter typed with a word processor was any less personal than one produced with a typewriter.

Fortunately the rumour began to circulate that Disraeli had used a WP and suddenly computers were 'in'. There's still a long way to go, but for both the major parties in the UK, computer campaigning in the constituencies is now widespread. With good software programmes and consistent input, a constituency can identify most of its own voters and potential switchers. Incidentally, much of the success of direct mail lies in the fact that, apart from bills, most of the population get no mail at all and people are delighted to get a letter that expresses interest in them, concern about them and opens the door for further contact and involvement.

It is not enough to notify the regional chairman or committee members of what's going on and hope that they will pass on the message to the members and supporters. (Remember the party game Chinese Whispers? The message comes out completely different at the other end.) The greater number of people who are well-briefed, the wider the cascade effect. Enthusiasm and commitment radiates outwards until it touches those on the edge of the circle and draws them in.

This is the way forward. A central core of keen and well-informed supporters whose enthusiasm, knowledge and confidence will draw new members like a magnet. Anything else is false economy.

Telephone campaigning

Telephone campaigning is an expanding field and one that can be very effective, but it is open to misuse; you can say almost anything on the telephone and campaigners have to be trained in the right technique. It should go without saying that an approach should be unfailingly courteous. Never preach, hector or bully. The wrong word can do your cause more harm than good.

The telephone can be rather cold as a method of first contact, but very useful if it is used in conjunction with a letter or a visit. In fact, the strongest impact is always made with three hits. So, for example, a letter and a phone call are good but a letter, a phone call and a visit even better.

This 'three hits' principle applies across the board in communication, but it takes effort.

Say, for instance, you're holding a press conference and you want to ensure maximum attendance. Send out an initial press notice. Find the name of the news editor or the particular specialist reporter and announce that you will be holding the conference to make a 'significant announcement'. Follow this 'teaser' with a second release giving full details of who, when and where, and follow it up again by a phone call checking that the right person has got the material.

The local scene

Local elections, however insignificant they might seem sometimes, are actually very important. They affect quite radically the life of a community and they have repercussions that reach up to national level. Local authorities can spoil or block what a government is trying to do, or they can steal its credit.

Political units overlap and influence each other. For example, if a local authority is apathetic about the European Community and the single market of 1992, they can effectively stifle interest and ensure a low turn-out for a European election. Equally, an authority that encourages exchange visits by schools, business and industry contacts, twinning with continental towns and so on, can easily raise the level of voter involvement.

In the United Kingdom there is no breathing space, no fallow time when a local party can sit back and not worry about politics. Elections of one kind or another are taking place three years out of four: parish, borough, county, European.

Contact does not have to be *political*; in fact it can be more effective when it isn't. A visit when someone is sick or an invitation to coffee is far more appreciated - and remembered - than a call to discuss committee problems. It's always the same principle: hearts first, then minds!

Setting goals

A local political organisation needs specific goals and a strategy. You need a measurable target.

If you are having a recruitment drive, decide what it is you want: 500 members in two years, 2,000 in five or whatever. I remember Billy Graham saying at Earls Court back in 1966 that the Christian Church in England should organise itself like the Communist Party: by forming active and multiplying cells, fixing a timetable, planning a strategy and working it through.

I keep hammering away at this point but it applies to so many areas and it's so rarely done. Good organisation is specific and detailed not bland and vague.

Your supporters

There are two types of supporter in politics. Those who want to be paid-up, signed-up members and those who for one reason or another do not actually want to become a member but are keen to be kept informed, involved and used as the occasion demands. So don't feel you've failed if people won't sign on the dotted line. They may turn out to be of equal value to those who do.

Some of the most effective recruitment campaigns I have worked with have been for limited commitment. Many people want to help but just don't want to be bogged down with wasteful committee meetings every week for years.

To involve people in Billy Graham Crusades we asked for a specific and limited commitment, something that people understood and could accept: a prayer meeting in their home once a week, *for five weeks only*; giving a monthly gift to the Crusade, *for six months only*. A finite contribution.

In local political organisation the technique is just as effective. By using it in Ealing in West London in 1979, we recruited enough help to win the borough council election and to take the parliamentary seat from Labour. Three hundred extra helpers were recruited to give eight hours help in the three months before the election, or two Saturday mornings, or four evenings in the final two months. The local constituency officers got new people and could plan how and when to use them - and later many of them decided they'd like to go on working with their new friends.

People and the community

Supporters of whatever political hue are people first and political creatures second. So if you approach a sympathetic, but so far neutral, person and start telling him that he ought to give his support because of x, y and z policies he is likely to be bored and irritated. But if you ask him to spare a couple of hours to help out at a St John Ambulance fund-raising activity or a garden fête for the church roof repair fund, he might find that a worthwhile thing to do. When he gets to the event and discovers that the people there are friendly, interesting and pleasant company - and most belong to the same political party - he will begin to think. You've caught his interest and got him involved by deeds more than words.

In grass roots politics interest grows mostly through non-party political activities. The Labour Party knows this and so do the Liberals (now Democrats) with their emphasis on community politics. It might seem little enough to get an extra bus stop or pedestrian crossing, but those are real concerns for local people and such matters affect the way they regard you politically.

Lord Cockfield, a European Commissioner from 1983 to 1988, discussed European publicity with me early in his term. He said: 'The most effective publicity we've ever had for the Community is the European Ryder Cup Golf Team. It means something for people to see the top golfers of the different nations playing together. It says more about the concept of the European Community than any amount of leaflets and party political broadcasts can.'

I'd like to see Euro MPs introducing their singers in the Eurovision Song Contest! Millions of people watch it, it involves and amuses them and it's the perfect forum for effective communication - not party political, just an idea of Europe.

But the best communication is always person to person. Let me give you an example. You know someone who you believe is a supporter and in conversation it's mentioned that he regularly gives to charities. You, if you are well informed, can then point out that there's a way in which he can get tax relief on his donations. Take the person the appropriate leaflet and explain the system. (You can see the need for good information to local constituency offices. If you are sent incomprehensible bumf, find someone locally who can translate it into readable English.) Your potential supporter is both helped and encouraged to look on your organisation more favourably because someone took time and trouble over him.

Once you have got a favourable response, you follow through with an invitation to a social event. Perhaps a letter from the local party chairman saying, 'I'm interested to learn you are a supporter of ours and I'd like the opportunity to get to know you. We're having a short breakfast-time get-together at 8:30 Saturday. We'll be serving scrambled eggs, toast and coffee - free of course - and we'll have the chance to chat.

We'll be through by 10:00 and you may find it interesting and useful. Do come along.'

The local media

You will not need telling that good relationships with your local press, radio and television are essential - but *how* do you do it?

First of all get to know them. Keep a complete list of all the reporting and editing staff on all the outlets in your area. Try to meet them in non-political situations and when you do not want anything from them. Take a school class or a group from your voluntary organisation to see how the local media work. Meet them with a local businessman or at other functions. When they know you, in a personal capacity, you have credibility when you contact them in a political role.

Second, never abuse that credibility. Make sure that the story you have for them is interesting and if it is merely constituency information, explain that you are providing it for background briefing and that you are not expecting them to publish it.

Many times over the years, I have contacted radio or television stations all over the world to propose a client to appear on a show. I have never suggested to the media that anybody goes on a programme, unless I know that it will be *good radio* or *good television*. My own professional credibility would be lost in an instant if I proposed a boring twit. On the other hand, if the media *ask* for someone to take part, try to make him or her as interesting as possible - for the programme not to themselves!

Third, make situations interesting. If your candidate is going to research the level of pollution in a local river, he doesn't stand on the bridge and look; he either wades in to feel for junk or he goes in with a professional diver to find it. In both cases it's a good story and photo; but in both cases make sure your candidate is properly equipped and safely escorted. 'Candidate disappears under junk in local river' is a bigger news story, but you lose the photo!

Fourth, don't always do a news release on all the grass roots activities. Sometimes, if you plan it, it's worth *not* reporting a newsworthy event - but make sure the local press finds out casually after it's over. Then *they come to you* (the third person principle) and ask you to make sure they are told of everything in future.

Fifth, be available. Make sure that all the local news people have the appropriate office and *home* phone numbers.

And finally, organise the volunteers to take part in phone-in radio programmes and write letters to both press and radio. *Do not wait for political discussions*. Get them to take part in all the community topics, but - and it's a big but - their opinions *must* be genuine. Don't plan twenty similar letters on one subject; your people lose credibility again. It is wise, however, to teach them the basics of radio and how to construct an *interesting* letter!

Advertising, publicity and public relations

Advertising, publicity and public relations all play a part in effective communication by local party organisations. Advertising is buying space in whatever medium and designing the selling device - poster, commercial, etc.

Publicity is the exposure you get by providing the resources yourself - leaflets, posters, press releases and newsworthy events - but the *space* is free. The leaflet and letter is posted through the door, the poster stuck up in the window, the story featured in the press.

Public relations or PR is slightly less visible. It is establishing and keeping up mutual understanding between an organisation and the people it wants to reach. It's the 'third person factor'.

'Marketing' incorporates all three. It means recognising or creating a need, pointing it out and offering to meet the need with your product or message.

What other people say about you - and your party - has far more impact than what you say about yourself. We're getting better at using this third person factor in political campaigning, but it's still not used fully. The reason why

EARLY CALL

Arrivals and departures can often be dramatic. I was travelling with President Carter's press corps in 1980. We had finished a big dinner in Chicago around midnight. Back at the O'Hare Airport Hilton we were told, 'The President's gone to bed. Nothing now until 0800.'

I fell into bed only to be woken by the telephone an hour later at 1.30am. 'Airforce One and Two will leave for Washington in one hour - please be downstairs in twenty minutes, packed.'

The President had seen the polls forecasting heavy defeat and had decided on a high-profile last-ditch effort to free the Iranian hostages. It didn't work but we all - or rather most of us - lost our sleep to fly in Airforce Two.

The following morning six of the travelling journalists showed up innocently for breakfast in Chicago wanting to know where everyone had gone. They had not been reachable when they were phoned in the night!

Governor Dukakis tried a similar dramatic stunt in 1988, holding midnight and early hour rallies for supporters between California and Boston on the last night of the campaign. That didn't work either, but it was imaginative and made the supporters feel better. In a very close race it just might have helped.

party political broadcasts, however clever and imaginative, rarely have a great impact is because they are still essentially advertising, and people know it. But when you get a senior foreign statesman commenting abroad how much the world respects Mrs Thatcher - that's a real PR coup.

The same principles work through the grass roots of a party. If you want to attract people to an event you will get a certain response by direct invitation, but a much greater rate of success when your members are saying: 'I'm going to a terrific do. So-and-so will be there, this-and-that will be happening - why don't you come with me?'

Meeting people

Once you've recruited your members and other helpers, you must use them and their talents.

One of the most important factors in any election campaign is finding out who is likely to vote for you - canvassing. It is a key task for your troops. They must find the information for you to base your strategy on. And gathering that information means knocking on doors and asking people questions. That awful script: 'Good morning/afternoon/evening. Have you decided which party you will vote for?'

Canvassing is usually done with a rather hit and miss approach. It is left to the individual's instinct and good sense, which are not always entirely sound. A Conservative candidate knocked at the door of a run-down council flat one evening at 7pm. The door was eventually opened by a scowling man, cigarette hanging from the corner of his mouth, towel around his waist, shaving soap on his face and a razor in his hand, getting ready for his night shift. The caller stepped back aghast and stuttered, 'I'm so sorry to disturb you - I see you're changing for dinner.'

There is an art to canvassing. Watch for tell-tale body language and gestures and give-away phrases in someone's response. If they know which party you are from and say, 'Oh I expect I'll vote for you', they probably mean 'I won't, but I want to get rid of you quickly because *Dallas* is just beginning', or 'I've no idea and I'm really not interested - politicians are all the same.'

Rather than marking the person down as a supporter, try a follow-up saying: 'Thanks, I'll get a colleague to call round.' If the response is, 'Oh, no it's alright, don't bother' - it's fair to assume you can't count on his vote.

Try to read the feedback and get as definite a picture as you can. You don't want to under- or over-estimate your strength. Canvassing is still done without uniformity of approach or agreed method and its results are often badly inaccurate. Canvassers should have training, which could in itself be fun for them. Get some volunteers to come and 'be canvassed' at a buffet supper. You might even win some supporters.

For some of us, meeting people is difficult but you do not have to be an outgoing, free and easy character in order to *learn* to meet and get on with new people. If you are involved with local politics, meeting people is going to be part of your task - unless you are ready to spend the whole time in a backroom stuffing envelopes.

Individually we are very much the same, but the circumstances that govern our lives might be quite different. Politics is about communicating with and winning a *person*, not winning an argument or battering home a policy line. When you first meet someone, assume you will meet them again. Take time to become acquainted. It will take more than one meeting and not all people are equally responsive. Try to be natural and objective. You will find it easier to talk to people if you don't take all their ideas personally. They have a right to think the way they do. When you know them better, by all means invite them to a party meeting but don't let your attitude to them be dependent on their political philosophy. As the initiator of the contact, the tone of the encounter, the degree of relaxation, ease and good humour, depends on you. If you handle it right your next contact will be easier.

All this is, I know, easier to say than to do and there are times when everyone feels shy. If you are nervous about meeting new people, take a friend with you on your first efforts. I am considered to be fairly outgoing but as a teenager I was painfully shy. I had to train myself to deal with people and situations and it's quite possible - once you make your mind up.

Meetings

Involvement with a political party will at some stage inevitably involve meetings. Like most other projects, meetings are not difficult to organise if you know the principles. I discussed them in some detail in the chapter on event planning.

There are four main points to remember: a clear objective, an overall picture of the event, meticulous preparation and the willingness to go an 'extra mile'.

Small meetings, regular get-togethers of people who mostly

know each other, are not so much my concern here, because they will probably run to an agreed format and be fairly self-contained. But anything of a bigger scale that involves attracting the public or rallying the faithful or listening to a guest speaker does need forethought and care if it is not to be a shambles.

If possible, visit your location weeks ahead, arrive hours before the meeting so that you can test your equipment and check through everything well before the doors open. Draw up a checklist to include: platform design and decoration, technical equipment, sound and lighting, stewards, signs, first aid arrangements, wheelchair space, press area, guest seating and parking. Don't be afraid to add your own items to the checklist; every meeting is different.

Always have a rehearsal and go through, on your own, every step. Check that you have the right information and equipment. Rehearsals save you being embarrassed in the meeting by broken light bulbs, out of focus films, a speaker half an hour late because he couldn't find anywhere to park, and shrieks and howls as the public address system does its best to drown the speaker.

Timing is critical: many meetings are marred by going on and on. Your audience must know that you finished on time, without knowing *how* you did it. Plan the schedule as a whole, and in detail, and write down exact timings. Always finish on time, unless there is a very good reason to overrun. Be flexible with the details so that if you are getting behind you can trim the programme. Brief your participants that you will be conducting the meeting this way and expect their co-operation. Leave them wanting more is a good piece of showbusiness advice. If people leave feeling it was good but rather long, you have failed. If they leave wishing it had gone on longer, you've succeeded.

If you are actually conducting a meeting, do it with sensitivity, objectivity, a cool head and an informal personal touch. Sometimes you can let the meeting carry on by itself - you don't have to bob up between every item on the programme. One person leading into another can make for a smoother flow and a more efficient use of time.

You're presenting a message, not hogging the limelight!

NIGHT TO FORGET

I remember one rally with Sir Geoffrey Howe (then Chancellor of the Exchequer) during the Crosby by-election near Liverpool in 1981. It was one of those disastrous meetings. The school caretaker hated the Tories so he locked everything except the loos (without drinking water) and the gym where the meeting was to be held. I had to jury-rig a public address system from a car amplifier with wires stretched, as I thought, out of the public's way to the side of the platform. Since I had no jugs, glasses or water I sent two elderly ladies out to knock on doors and borrow some - assuming they could find a friendly Conservative nearby.

I hurriedly put on a music tape at twenty to eight to keep the packed crowd of 450 reasonably settled. At ten to eight, before the platform party arrived, I walked into the auditorium to find the entire crowd standing stiffly to attention as my marching music tape played the National Anthem, which I hadn't noticed was on it!

Sir Geoffrey and the others arrived at five to eight. The room by now was steaming hot and there was no water on the top table. The chairman, without so much as a by-your-leave to me, said to all the young people, 'You're so crowded sitting back there, why don't you come and sit here on the floor around the platform?' A hundred of them did so and bust every microphone wire that I had in the process.

Sir Geoffrey stood up to speak with no water and no PA system. Five minutes into the speech the two elderly ladies came slowly down the aisle with a jug of water and some glasses, and Sir Geoffrey graciously stopped in full flow to thank them and have a chat before struggling on with no microphone.

A year later he used my hydraulic lectern at the Brighton Party Conference and as he came off stage he said to me, with his wonderfully dry sense of humour, 'It's so nice to find a gadget of yours that actually works, Harvey.'

I'm sure it was purely coincidence that we lost that by-election to Shirley Williams . . .

10
ON THE ROAD

You should never put on your best trousers when you go out to fight for freedom and truth.

Henrik Ibsen

On the wall of our dining room is one of my favourite pictures - a composite photograph of all of the 'Roadies' team for Mrs Thatcher's 1987 election tour. It's a favourite because it reminds me of the most exciting part of political campaigning: the roadshow.

That's where the politicians meet the people and the adrenalin really flows in those exhilerating, nervewracking, exhausting three to four weeks before polling day. You've got your candidate, you've got a date, you've got your strategy and organisation and now you've got to put theory into practice. The roadshow team has to put it all together - and win.

In spite of all the technological developments and the sophistication and speed of modern communication, the point of a campaign roadshow is the same as it was in the days of the whistle-stop tour when politicians addressed voters from the backs of trains: to communicate with the maximum number of people in the short time available.

Being on the road is the lifeblood of politics and that's something that these days television enhances, because whatever the potential of studio interviews or recorded broadcasts, some of the most effective television comes from live campaigning 'out there'.

An imaginative on-the-road campaign involves all kinds of activity: walkabouts, whistle-stop tours, visits to places of interest, speeches delivered in market places, shops, factories, farms and building sites. It can cover anything from giving a church sermon to holding a mass rally. What unites all these disparate activities is that they all help to maximise the impact and outreach of your message, to present the person or the party in the most effective way to enthuse and woo the voters. Interest - inform - involve. These are the aims.

The message comes first

Presentation is a growing profession and business, as we come to the nineties. It is interesting and perhaps unusual that it developed first in politics but now is used more and more in commerce and industry. The explosion of television outlets has been a key factor in this trend.

Isaiah wrote that whenever the Bible, as the Word of God, was proclaimed it would 'never return void'. In other words the message itself would always have an effect. Even so, it is clear that the most effective proclaimers of the Gospel are those who have learned how to speak and present their message professionally.

I would not presume to add anything to the Word of God but I have a sneaking suspicion that if Isaiah had been writing in the 1990s he might have added a phrase. He might have said for example: 'The Word shall never return void but its impact will be a whole lot greater if it's presented well.'

Of course, before you start reaching out to others you have to get your own act together.

Mid-term between the 1983 and 1987 General Elections I had lunch with a friend, the film producer David Wickes. At the time the Conservatives were low in the polls and within the Party the various political and organisational groups were not yet pulling hard together towards the election. I mentioned some of the problems we were facing and David asked, 'Harvey, do your people actually *want* to win the next election?'

As I thought about that perceptive question I realised its implications. Was the message or the product *important* enough to present properly? Did the result *matter* to those of us who were involved? And if it *was* important, to us and the country, why in the world weren't we snuffing out all those niggling grievances and getting on with the job of winning?

It's only when you've put yourself second and the message first that you can get on with the business of communication.

On-the-road campaigning allows the repetition of a simple theme to different live audiences. This theme, illustrated in all kinds of ways, is then thrust home to millions more by television. The roadshow's organiser must always keep this larger audience in mind. Those who are not on the spot will get their impressions firstly through television and radio coverage and then through newspapers. So you must not get bogged down in detail. Remember the importance of the visual image and try to keep your theme unified and simple. Avoid the detail that could divide, and hammer home the principles that unite.

There has been a lot of debate in political circles as to whether on-the-road campaigning should tackle political issues or concentrate on displaying the personality of the candidates. Obviously I'm not saying that political issues should not be debated. Indeed the political theme for the day should be set at the morning's press conferences, and local candidates and VIPs fully briefed and able to talk about or answer questions on that topic wherever they may be. What such issues must not do is clog up the wheels: travelling communications must have clarity and cohesion. Above all they must have punch.

And beware of flogging an issue too hard. Sometimes it sounds like a good idea to tackle, say, health or education all through one day on the road, in a particular area. In practice it's often very hard to sustain. There is, after all, a limit to the number of schools or hospitals in a town that you can go to without everyone getting bored or the whole business seeming increasingly contrived. At the end of the day it is the *person* that makes the impact.

The right place, the right time

A lot of the work in this field is logistical: getting the right people to the right place at the right time with the right equipment. Because time is short you will want to fit in as much as possible without over-reaching yourself. In other words aim for targets that are possible but only just. Don't try to cover Berlin,

Hamburg and Munich or Paris, Strasbourg and Marseilles or London, Plymouth and Glasgow in one day, however good you are with plane schedules and grass landing strips.

On the last day of the 1988 American presidential election Dukakis went on a whirlwind tour that must have been dreamed up by a desperate team. He crossed the country from California to Massachusetts - with rallies en route - in twelve hours. There should be no need for that!

Use a logical progression or a system radiating out from a central base. It is less demanding on the people involved and offers less chance of something going drastically wrong.

Sometimes there is no special political reason for going to a place. It's simply that people need to see their leaders and would feel hurt if they believed themselves forgotten. Of course one must put a lot of effort into marginal seats, but in the long term you must not forget the safe ones too. Besides, you need to motivate workers in safe seats to go and help in the others.

You must also be sensitive to the special needs and preoccupations of a particular area and its people. Britain is a richly varied country and the politician you are presenting must be well briefed about these local concerns before he or she arrives. On the other hand you don't want to get too embroiled in parochial issues if you are hoping to attract national coverage. It's a question of getting the balance right and doing your homework.

Keeping the media happy

Sometimes the needs of local and national media conflict. The first needs a strong local angle of interest to its community, the other something that can hold its own against all the other stories of the day. It takes skill and judgement and sometimes a compromise is not possible - you may have to choose one over the other.

I had a difficult time at one airport on a visit during the 1987 election.

The national press and media were travelling on the plane with Mrs Thatcher, but the local photographers and journalists were going directly to the airport ahead of time. Once they got there, however, they found the police would not allow them onto the tarmac with the welcoming VIPs and it looked at one point as though they were not going to get any pictures.

A bit of discreet negotiating sorted it out and the area chairman led Mrs Thatcher over to have a word with the local press on her way to the Battlebus, as we called the campaign coach. But if we had not been advancing properly - being there just ahead of the main party to iron out any difficulties - the result could have been a very serious error in terms of local coverage, with potentially unhappy consequences.

When you are planning a schedule you should also bear in mind the location of speeches and statements. Geography is usually irrelevant, but not always. For instance, if you are going to be discussing inner city problems, speaking about them from a beautiful stately home deep in the heart of the countryside lessens the impact somewhat!

Don't lose sight of the candidate

Whatever your programme, certain basic rules must be obeyed. They are so basic they seem obvious, yet it's amazing how often they are broken or ignored. First and foremost everyone present at an event must be able to see and hear, and the press must be able to see and hear slightly better than the rest without getting in the way of the guests. (Incidentally never forget to plan for the practical needs of the press when you're drawing up your arrangements. We always provide telephone or fax facilities and try to schedule events to fit deadlines.)

I'd even go a step further than the physical necessities of being able to see and hear properly and say that the audience must be in the right mood, too, to receive the message.

The candidate must not be hidden in or by the crowd; at the same time he must not appear too remote. If you put someone on a second floor balcony, for instance, to deliver an address, it looks as if he is simply haranguing his listeners. In the Portuguese elections of 1984, where I was an adviser, it was quite a problem - it had always been done from the second floor - so I suggested the flatbed truck concept that had been so successful in Malta.

I campaigned there in 1981 for Eddie Fenech-Adami. He is now Prime Minister but was then Leader of the Opposition. The rallies were wonderful affairs. For most of them the 'arena' was formed just by swinging a huge articulated truck across one end of the street. The street then became the stadium and the custom-built truck opened out into a full stage with a public address system, railings, lights, flags, party backdrop and seating all built in.

Although it looked completely different, it was this truck that gave me the concept for 'MiniMag', the 27ft (8m) articulated truck that we used for Mrs Thatcher's open-air meetings in the 1987 election. We used to drive it into fields or parking lots and open it up to reveal a complete Conservative campaign stage. It had everything we could think of - lights, PA system, lectern and its own generator. The slogan at the back of the stage could be changed so that the appropriate place name could be inserted according to where we were.

It meant we could have a sophisticated presentation platform literally in the middle of nowhere and people came from miles around for these outdoor meetings.

There were occasions when we couldn't use it: instead we had to rely on our improvisation skills.

Once we did not know where the Battlebus was going to stop during a tour of Suffolk until minutes before it arrived. In that short interval we managed to grab a couple of milk crates and a door that we found at the edge of a building site. We stapled a piece of blue baize around the door and, hey presto, there was a neat little portable platform which we could produce when the time came, looking incredibly efficient.

Another day we had an open-air meeting in a field by a river near Southampton Airport. My helpers borrowed an old flatbed truck from a farmer, along with two dozen squared bales of hay which they arranged as steps leading up to the truck. They then commandeered a battery operated amplifier and two loudspeakers from the local constituency association, and via the roof of one of their cars set up an excellent PA system.

By the time the guest arrived in the field there was a platform made of wooden beams and corrugated iron, a vantage point for the press and the necessary amplification. Everyone enjoyed the pleasant outdoor atmosphere and setting without having to forfeit convenience. I think they thought those structures had been there forever.

LATE ARRIVAL

You must always be ready to think on your feet.

In Eddie Fenech-Adami's final rally in Malta in 1981 we had the old stadium in Valetta. A capacity crowd of 40,000 turned up. We expected sabotage from the Labour extremists and hired two 100,000 watt generators in case the electrical sub-station was cut off. As it turned out the problem came not from the Opposition but from our own side.

After a one-and-a-half-hour pop concert the political programme began. We had all the leading Maltese Nationalists to speak, not to mention two former Italian prime ministers. All we lacked was Eddie Fenech-Adami. We tried frantically to reach him with our walkie-talkies, but he was somewhere en route from the island of Gozo. In desperation I said to Noel Buttigieg-Scicluna, Secretary of the Maltese Nationalist Party, 'Noel, please go up and make a speech until we can find Eddie.'

Noel ran onto the platform and said: 'The last ex-Italian prime minister's speech was so good I'm going to repeat it in Maltese to make sure you don't miss any of it.' And he did.

He finished just as Eddie arrived. We swung into the Brotherhood of Man's special theme tune and turned all the spots on the stadium entrance. We just saw Eddie's tiny figure coming through the entrance in an open Land Rover before we collapsed in hysterical relief.

Incidentally, the Maltese have a delightful habit of carrying their political leaders by hand over the heads of the crowd. I once saw Eddie travel nearly half a mile like that. It's not quite as effective as walking on water, but it comes close. You cannot see the bearers until they are right by you so the effect is of the person floating on air as he passes along the heads of the crowd and leans over to shake hands.

It's not, however, very practical for most countries - or most politicians!

Plan A and Plan B

I mentioned the vital importance of site visits in the conference section, but it applies equally in roadshow campaigning. You *must* visit *every* spot ahead of time to plan what you are actually going to do on the day with your candidate or leader. Of course, having worked out this wonderful plan, you will probably have to create another one on that day because of some unforeseen circumstance.

I was recently involved with a stone-laying ceremony for a new school. We checked out the site a week beforehand. The field lay alongside a road in a London suburb and we thought that people could stand on the road and look across six metres into the field to the platform where the ceremony would take place.

On the day, however, we discovered that the level of the field had dropped by two metres. Thousands of tons of earth had been moved as part of the site development.

There was absolutely no point in having two hundred people perched up on the road looking down on the top of a marquee. In three hours we managed to get the contractors to build an earth ramp, roll it flat, cover it with gravel and put a handrail alongside so that people could walk down from the road to a flat area beside the ceremony site.

A colleague said, 'Now I know what it means to move mountains.'

At times like that you do your initial planning only to find that everything has changed and you have to fly by the seat of your pants. Nonetheless, start out with a master plan and wherever possible, use it.

Because you need to get maximum use of your time in an on-the-road campaign a last minute change, even a small one, can have immense repercussions. It can even jeopardise the whole operation.

During the 1987 election we set a carefully timed and organised arrival at a particular airport. The seventy strong press and media corps were in the rear of the Prime Minister's plane and we had arranged a special area and platform for them in the terminal. That way they would get excellent pictures of Mrs Thatcher as she moved through the crowd.

For this to work though, it was absolutely essential to get them to their spot a minute or two ahead of her, and to achieve that we had arranged for Mrs Thatcher to pause for a cup of coffee with the VIPs in a small room just outside the terminal door. The object was not to provide refreshment but to hold up the party for two or three minutes in order to get the press into position. Unfortunately for our timing one of the hosts suddenly said, 'I'm sure you don't want any coffee, Prime Minister, you've just come off the plane. Let's go straight through.' And with that took Mrs Thatcher's arm and led her off.

The result was chaos. There was no way the press could catch up, let alone get in position ahead. The airport became a free-for-all with the journalists charging after Mrs Thatcher, battling to get a good shot and knocking people in the crowd over in the process.

That mix-up caused us serious problems for the rest of the campaign because we had to be constantly reassuring the media that we would get them good positions. Because they had been confused and upset early on in the campaign they found it hard to relax and trust us.

Opportunity knocks

When I talk about positions and opportunities for pictures I don't suggest that you can plan them all. Part of the presenter's role is to watch for good photo opportunities as they arise spontaneously in the course of events. Obviously situations like the airport arrival can be worked out ahead of time and you can plan how best to accommodate the media for such moments, but it's equally important to spot new potential and make the most of it.

Don't try and set up something that is quite patently false. Everyone will be embarrassed and it rarely helps. At the same time, on-the-road campaigning will produce its own moments so you have to know your candidate and know your location. You cannot, for instance, turn someone into a surfing champion just because he's at the seaside, but if it turns out that he has a genuine interest in fishing and some skills as a fisherman you can centre pictures and film on that. Because it's genuine, it looks good.

When you are looking for such opportunities, however, beware of allowing visual images to blind you to potential problems. For instance, we were making a film about how well a particular local authority was doing and we were planning to shoot the thundering morning turn-out of dozens of heavy cleaning trucks at five o'clock in the morning.

It turned out that all the big trucks were Volvos, so in order to keep things British we had to confine our film to little electric dustcarts. Not nearly so visually impressive but essential content-wise.

By the way, always make sure you've cleared all on-the-road activities with the necessary authorities. You don't want your brilliant impromptu inspiration to get you into trouble.

Sound, as well as visual image, plays a big part in successful campaigning: applause, off-the-cuff conversations, speeches, music and cheering. And spontaneous ad-libs are great - as long as they're properly rehearsed.

Remember, people are interested in people not politics and the best campaign moments are those with a human touch.

At the same time allow for human frailties. The person you depend on can lose his or her nerve about something which seems straightforward, like presenting a bunch of flowers or offering a cup of tea. All can seem well till the last moment. Then they see the size of the crowd or the famous VIP arriving and they are overwhelmed with terror.

I remember going to a fruit and flower market in Leeds very early one morning during a tour and one of the staff was going to bring a cup of tea and a bacon buttie to Mrs Thatcher. In the end the man became so nervous that I had to hold his arm and literally steer him through the crowd to the right spot. Because of the mystique - and maybe the image - celebrities and VIPs are quite daunting to those who usually only see them from a distance. I'm not quite sure why. How often I have heard the amazement in someone's voice: 'You know, he actually wanted the loo!' Human after all!

Security

Security is a major headache these days. It means, for instance, that you cannot announce the whereabouts of major political figures in advance which makes your presentation via the media even more crucial: sometimes they are the only people you can take into a particular venue. Even where you have more flexibility, such as constituency campaigning by local candidates, you may still need to choose your audiences and visitors carefully. And you have to be careful that there are not so many policemen round your VIPs that the real people - the public - don't get to see them.

There is no national police authority in the United Kingdom as there is with the FBI in America, for example. Each of our forces is autonomous and has a different approach to security. You have to liaise with them on policy and practicalities.

ECHO FROM THE PAST

In 1980 Marlies and I spent three days travelling with Senator Edward Kennedy in his motorcade during the presidential primary campaign. We were with his secretary in the car immediately behind the gun car, a huge open station wagon with six secret service men wearing bullet-proof jackets and with the most vicious looking automatic rifles at the ready. All the motorways were cleared and our sixteen car motorcade cruised down the centre of the freeway at 60mph.

The next day Kennedy was addressing a meeting in a black church in Los Angeles. As he began to speak a young boy ran straight through a plate glass window behind us at the back of the church.

The glass exploded with a loud shot-like crack. It was seventeen years after President Kennedy's assassination, twelve years since Bobby's, but the idea was so powerful nobody turned to look at the shattered window or the stunned lad. Every eye was on Edward Kennedy. Had he been shot?

There was no need for anyone to say the words. The pastor spoke first: 'It's all right. The Senator is not hurt.' Only then did everyone turn and pay attention to the boy and the window behind them.

In 1985 in Washington DC I was responsible for the security co-ordination of eleven prime ministers and twenty other Conservative party leaders from around the world who were there for the International Democrat Union Party Leaders' meeting. I worked with the FBI, the US Secret Service, the thirty-one diplomatic groups and the individual protection teams. There were fascinating differences of approach from the White House to Paris, from Oslo to Bonn, from Tokyo to Canberra. At first I had visions of an OK Corral shoot-out at High Noon between dozens of different security forces who didn't know each other, but in fact we worked it out and there were no serious problems.

One of the effects of this increased need for security has been to strengthen the importance of the big set-piece occasions like rallies where access can be controlled and crowds organised.

French farce

An election rally must inspire, enthuse and excite, and radiate these qualities out through the media. The atmosphere must be right *in* the arena and the whole event must be properly produced and co-ordinated. Individuals doing their own thing does not work, as Jacques Chirac found out at a 1988 Paris rally.

There was lots of very French glitz and glamour and an apparently unlimited budget, much of which had been spent on giant television screens and clever use of lights; but it was all quite impractical and unco-ordinated. Nobody seemed to have a clear objective in mind and the speakers had obviously not been briefed on what to expect.

Some basic rules were broken. Most of the 25,000 audience in the Palais Bercy could not see the platform because of the enormous scaffold bridge built across it for the cameras. The bridge was too high for a good angle anyway and the fact that it blocked the view of so many meant that the atmosphere never developed properly, so that the cameras had nothing to convey. It was a vicious circle.

Politics were allowed to intrude too much: in fact they spoiled the rally. Chirac had to be seen to be making concessions to his defeated rival Le Barre in order to get Le Barre's support for the run-off against Mitterand. So both men were given almost equal prominence and Le Barre virtually killed off any audience interest with a heavy speech.

Chirac didn't even know where to go while Le Barre was speaking on an empty white platform with no chairs, and when it was his turn to speak he had no chance of a good clean start because he had to shake hands with Le Barre as they passed on the stairs. It was a study in how not to do something and it cost Chirac dear.

Gofers

However, back to roadshow campaigning and an important innovation: Gofers.

I introduced the concept to this country during the 1987 General Election in an attempt to overcome one of the major difficulties facing campaign organisers: getting consistent standards of presentation. Up until then it had been virtually impossible. Local staff or voluntary workers cannot be expected to have the resources, time or experience to ensure that telecommunications, backdrop, crowd flow, music, lighting and camera positions are available at the right time and in the right way. Travelling teams of Gofers can.

A 'Gofer' is not the little squirrel-like animal of the American Midwest, although there is a certain behavioural resemblance, but an abbreviation of 'Go-for a coffee', 'Go-for a piece of string' etc. (Actually I originally decided to call the teams Oyus as in 'Oi you, go for some coffee'.) We recruited a team of twenty-five young executives whose firms or colleagues gave them three weeks paid leave for the election campaign.

It's a concept I adapted from the American presidential campaigns. We'd had a huge rally of 10,000 people for Ronald Reagan at the Southern Methodist University in Dallas and I was flying on to Los Angeles with one of the co-ordinators the next morning. I asked him how long he had been with the Republicans and he said, 'Three weeks - I'm a sales manager and I've been given leave of absence by my company just to produce last night's rally.'

Our 1987 Gofers were terrific. They were invaluable to our road campaign and it was a great and new experience for them. We had barristers and solicitors, merchant bankers, sales and advertising executives, a restaurant manager, researchers, a public relations officer, a textile broker and farmers among the team. Their average age was about twenty-five.

They had to be ready - and able - to do absolutely anything from greeting a minister off a plane to cleaning drains, from handling the press to guiding the helicopter down to its landing site with hand signals. Because they were already in successful careers they were able to learn fast and by the second week our Gofer teams were veteran roadies.

We needed a Gofer to drive 'MiniMag' around the country and I asked if anyone could drive articulated lorries. One girl volunteered with confidence and handled the vehicle without trouble during the campaign. I was a little concerned though when the makers of 'MiniMag' asked what experience she'd had of articulated vehicles and she replied, 'I've spent my life driving Daddy's horse-boxes.'

On another occasion we were meeting the Prime Minister's plane at Cardiff Airport, with only two Gofers in the team that day. We had lost the press buses and one of the Gofers, a merchant banker, came up to me on the tarmac to ask if I knew where they were.

The man standing by my side said that he had seen them behind the terminal. Our Gofer (a young woman) grabbed his hand before I could say anything and said, 'Great, show me will you?' and dashed off with him in tow, coats flying. We would have actually liked to have told her that the man was the Secretary of State for Wales and a member of the Cabinet! Still they returned safely with the press buses.

Four minutes later I had another nervous moment. I asked her to meet the press off the back of the BAC One-Eleven as it came to a stop in front of us. She shot off looking up at the plane, underneath the tail and far wing and back again. As a successful merchant banker there was no reason for her to know where the back door was in a BAC One-Eleven, and that the tail opened downwards with the stairs!

By the last of the three weeks the Gofer teams were performing brilliantly. They had learned the principles and techniques necessary to focus all the attention onto the VIPs, and to make it easy for presenters, audiences and the news media. The use of Gofers in 1987 was a successful pioneer effort. They were the right sort of people - talented and with some experience, and willing to get their hands dirty.

Efficient management of the political parties in the nineties cannot carry permanent numbers of young professionals whose talents are so necessary in major campaigns. The Gofer concept provides good mobile flexible staff help, just for the times it is needed. It gives valuable experience to the Gofers, which is usually translated into a more effective contribution to their own work when they return to it. And it allows companies both to contribute to and benefit from election campaigns.

I want to take the Gofer idea a little further here based on a primary principle of presentation.

A 'sales pitch', a campaign of any kind, an annual general meeting, must never be 'produced' by the VIPs, the candidate or the sales team themselves. They must be presented, minded and mollycoddled if necessary so that they concentrate totally on their own performance.

Unfortunately senior executives often either consider that no-one less senior than themselves can be trusted with knowledge of a meeting, or that the meeting is so important that they alone are significant enough to occupy the chair. This is merely routine arrogance, but it obscures from them the fact that they could impress everyone a lot more if they could do a better job - and with a bit of help they could.

If you are pitching for an account, appearing on television or radio, making a significant speech, always have a company Gofer with you. This is never extravagant. It is just an extension of on-the-road campaigning.

Consider this scenario which I see consistently two or three times a year. You and your colleagues arrive to present a pitch for an advertising account. You are going to use a video and some slides on a little portable projector. You are following two other companies and the last one is moving their equipment out as you come into the room.

CAR PHONES

Mobile phones have changed on-the-road campaigning drama- tically, and for the better. I wonder how on earth we worked the 1979 and 1983 elections without them.

At one point in 1987 I was bowling up the M6 talking to a colleague in London on my 'hands-off' Cellnet phone - it had a microphone in front of me on the visor. My assistant Joanne Barker was talking on her phone and two more colleagues were in the back seat on their phones.

When my own hand mobile rang Joanne answered: 'I'm sorry, Harvey's on his other line and our three phones are all occupied. Could he call you back? He should be free by Wigan.' All at 69mph on the motorway. I hope the caller was impressed. I certainly was!

Another time in the 1987 election we were driving along a dual carriageway in Norfolk heading for an airport to meet Mrs Thatcher's plane and join up with the Battlebus. We thought all was well until the Battlebus passed us at full speed in the opposite direction. Since both of us were going to meet the same plane, one of us was definitely going the wrong way. We telephoned from our mobile to theirs - probably at a combined speed of 100mph going away from each other - and it was indeed us who were hotfooting it away from the airport. We made it on time - just - thanks to our car phones.

A final story about these phones. Joanne had handled the set- up of the press conference in Glasgow and I had gone on to Newcastle Airport to meet the plane there. Early fog had cleared and the airport manager and I were standing on the tarmac lining up the motorcade when my car phone rang. It was Joanne on Mrs Thatcher's plane at Glasgow Airport. 'The pilot has just said we're diverting to Teeside because of the fog at Newcastle - we're taxiing out now,' she said.

I relayed the message to the airport manager who rushed to the control tower just in time to contact the pilot and air traffic control to say that Newcastle Airport was open and all was OK. That's good on-the-road (or on-the-tarmac) thinking.

Confidently you open your portable projector and put it on the table. Then it hits you - your power line isn't long enough and you haven't checked the video and TV (if they are there at all).

The table is a five-metre boardroom piece. You can't move it. You ask for an extension lead. There isn't one. You ask for a chair and four telephone directories and rig up an impromptu table near the only plug - and ask all your prospective clients to turn their heads around.

Someone gets strangled in the wire and pulls out the plug. Your concentration and your confidence has been lost. You are sweating and grubby. Your chance of the contract has gone - along with the picture from your video cassette.

What you needed was a Gofer: someone who had nothing else to do but look after you and your team. He would have checked your equipment in advance, brought extension lead and table, checked the video on that particular TV and set it all up while you were shaking hands and making conversation rather than getting flustered.

When you came to make your presentation he would even have put a glass of water within reach in case you needed it - *and* operated the equipment for you.

That's what I mean by attention to detail. Good Gofers can save face, time and trouble and allow *you* to make an impact.

Above all, campaigning must be fun for watchers and participants. It should be different, out of the ordinary, exciting.

I suppose that the common denominator in on-the-road campaigning is the commitment it requires, especially from the volunteer workers in the constituencies who make the biggest sacrifice. They have to keep the rest of their work and life going as well as helping the Party. Their reward is often in the hands of those of us who are campaigning professionals. In this instance the objective is not just a winning result; it is also to leave the volunteer workers with an awareness not only of their importance, but of the value of the contribution they have made and how much they are appreciated by the 'roadies' and the candidates passing through.

A pig and a chicken were walking together and they saw a huge sign advertising scrambled eggs and bacon. 'Awful isn't it?' said the chicken. 'Listen,' said the pig, 'for you it's just an offering - for me it's a real sacrifice'.

LAST WORDS

Advice is seldom welcome, and those who want it the most, always like it the least.
4th Earl of Chesterfield

In 1980 I set out to change the face of political presentation in the UK and to use some of these new concepts and techniques in business and industry as well.

With a lot of help from other people I believe we've done just that. Much of the time the principal performers were not even aware of what we were doing for them. But today, a decade later, the art and profession of presentation is recognised as an essential strategic ingredient for making an impact in communications.

Success in this field is going to become even more important as we move into the 1990s and beyond and I hope that in this book I've been able to give you the benefit of my experience, to pass on the kind of backstage know-how that can make that vital difference between winning and losing.

But I also hope I've done something else. I hope I've given you the motivation - and confidence - to go out and develop your own personal communication style to its full potential.

I leave you with my ten basic 'commandments of presentation'. As Sherlock Holmes said to Dr Watson, 'You know my methods: apply them.'

TEN COMMANDMENTS

1 See yourself as you really are

2 Know your objective

3 Have an overall picture in mind before you start on the details

4 Work out your route plan

5 Rehearse

6 Take your audience by the hand and lead them along with you

7 Win hearts - then minds

8 Keep it simple

9 Be enthusiastic

10 Be yourself

INDEX

Index

Index

Index

ADVICE FROM THE TOP
Business Strategies of Britain's Corporate Leaders
Derek Ezra and David Oates

Derek Ezra introduces *Advice From The Top* in which twelve of our most distinguished internationally-renowned business leaders talk frankly about how they handle the key aspects of running a successful business: social responsibility, teamwork, delegation, strategic planning, and dealing with crises. Revealed here are the strategies and attitudes which have taken them to the top of their industries and have kept them there – in some cases for thirty years or more.

Corporate leadership has become a demanding way of life, calling for the rare and valued qualities of resilience and patience. Each of the contributors to this thought-provoking book has three qualities in abundance, and their experiences will be both a practical help and an inspiration to those who aspire to following in their footsteps.

The contributors are: Sir Adrian Cadbury; Sir Terence Conran; Sir John Cuckney; Sir Monty Finniston; Sir Robert Haslam; Sir Hector Laing; Sir Austin Pearce; Anita Roddick; Peter de Savary; Sir Adam Thomson; Sir Francis Tombs and Sir Graham Wilkins.

AVOIDING ADVERSITY
How Insiders and Outsiders Can Avoid and Detect Business Failure
Bill Houston

Why do apparently healthy businesses fail? Can anything be done to rescue them? Or to avoid the crisis in the first place?

A corporate crisis is seldom unexpected by those who can read the signals, and in this timely book, *Bill Houston*, a specialist in corporate turnaround work, shows you how to recognise the signs of failure and what avoiding action to take. The book is divided into four parts: Part 1 covers the task of turning the company around, Part 2 shows how to strengthen the balance sheet, Part 3 is devoted to a new approach to reducing fixed costs, and Part 4 shows how to assemble information and put it into a wider context for people outside the company.

Whether you are involved in company rescue or are simply concerned with the fate of a particular company, whether you are a banker, an accountant, a shareholder, an employee, a trading partner or a journalist, this is the ideal handbook for anyone interested in corporate failure and how to avoid it.

THE 20% FACTOR

The Key to Personal and Corporate Success

Graham Lancaster

A must for all company libraries! *The 20% Factor* is the latest book from the chairman and chief executive of Biss Lancaster, a leading UK PR company which is part of one of the world's largest communications groups. Drawing on his experience as policy advisor to the CBI, Graham Lancaster claims that individuals can improve both their personal and corporate performance by twenty per cent almost immediately by taking some simple steps to understand and utilise image-making, establish good personal contacts and develop public relations.

Written in an intelligent and entertaining manner, the book uses a mixture of successful techniques to enable readers and their organisations to monitor their performance more effectively than ever before.

GETTING THROUGH

How to Make Words Work

Godfrey Howard

This is the book which brought together some of the most intelligent people in the world, when it was chosen as a theme for the international MENSA conference at Queen's College, Cambridge. In this remarkable rewrite the book now launches invaluable advice for communication into the 1990s.

This is what they said about the first edition:

'If you want to get a job interview, ask for a raise, propose marriage or seduction, write a compelling sales letter or create a great advertisement, read this book first. It will focus your mind wonderfully.'

Saatchi & Saatchi

'*Getting Through* is such an inspiration. Apart from practising what it teaches, recommending it at every lecture on communication and using it as a map, I have finally used it as a theme for the international MENSA conference . . .'

John McNulty, MENSA committee

'I find it fascinating. Every school leaver should buy a copy, read it – and give it to their parents.'

John Whitney, Director General, Independent Broadcasing Authority